Cambridge First Certificate in English 3 & 4

TEACHER'S BOOK

Examination papers from the University of Cambridge Local Examinations Syndicate

CAMBRIDGE
UNIVERSITY PRESS

PUBLISHED BY THE PRESS SYNDICATE OF THE UNIVERSITY OF CAMBRIDGE
The Pitt Building, Trumpington Street, Cambridge, United Kingdom

CAMBRIDGE UNIVERSITY PRESS
The Edinburgh Building, Cambridge CB2 2RU, UK
40 West 20th Street, New York, NY 10011–4211, USA
477 Williamstown Road, Port Melbourne, VIC 3207, Australia
Ruiz de Alarcón 13, 28014 Madrid, Spain
Dock House, The Waterfront, Cape Town 8001, South Africa

http://www.cambridge.org

First published 2002
Reprinted 2002

Printed in the United Kingdom at the University Press, Cambridge

ISBN 75088 1 Student's Book 3 & 4
ISBN 75089 X Teacher's Book 3 & 4

Also available:
ISBN 58726 3 Student's Book 3
ISBN 79771 3 Student's Book 3 with answers
ISBN 58725 5 Teacher's Book 3
ISBN 58724 7 Cassette Set (Book 3)

ISBN 64640 5 Student's Book 4
ISBN 79770 5 Student's Book 4 with answers
ISBN 64639 1 Teacher's Book 4
ISBN 64638 3 Cassette Set (Book 4)

Contents

Introduction

The level of FCE

The First Certificate in English (FCE) offers an intermediate-level qualification for those wishing to use English for professional, social or study purposes. In order to take into account developments in language teaching and testing, the FCE examination was revised in December 1996.

FCE candidates

In 2000, there were approximately 260,000 candidates for FCE throughout the world. Candidates come from a wide range of backgrounds and take the examination for a number of different reasons. The following points summarise the characteristics of the current FCE candidature.

Nationality

FCE is taken by candidates throughout the world in about 100 countries, although the total number of nationalities represented in the candidature is over 150. The majority of these candidates enter for FCE in European and South American countries.

Age and gender

Most candidates (about 75%) are under 25, with the average age being about 22. In some countries the average age is lower (e.g. in Greece it is about 17 years old). About 65% of candidates are female.

Employment

Most candidates are students, although there are considerable differences in the proportion of students in different countries.

Exam preparation

A large proportion of candidates (about 80%) undertake a preparatory course before taking the examination; most of these courses last between 8 and 24 weeks.

Reasons for taking FCE

Candidates' reasons for wanting an English-language qualification are roughly distributed as follows:

- to gain employment (37%)
- out of personal interest (33%)
- for further study (30%)

The structure of FCE: *an overview*

UCLES (University of Cambridge Local Examinations Syndicate) has developed a series of examinations with similar characteristics spanning five levels. Within the series of five levels, the First Certificate in English is at Cambridge Level Three:

Cambridge Level 5 Certificate of Proficiency in English (CPE)
Cambridge Level 4 Certificate of Advanced English (CAE)
Cambridge Level 3 First Certificate in English (FCE)
Cambridge Level 2 Preliminary English Test (PET)
Cambridge Level 1 Key English Test (KET)

The FCE examination consists of five papers:

Paper 1	**Reading**	1 hour 15 minutes
Paper 2	**Writing**	1 hour 30 minutes
Paper 3	**Use of English**	1 hour 15 minutes
Paper 4	**Listening**	40 minutes (approximately)
Paper 5	**Speaking**	14 minutes (approximately)

Paper 1   Reading

Candidates are expected to be able to read semi-authentic texts of various kinds (informative and general interest) and to show understanding of gist, detail and text structure, and to deduce meaning.

The paper contains four parts and 35 questions. Each part contains a text and corresponding comprehension tasks. Part 4 may contain two or more shorter related texts.

Paper 2   Writing

Candidates are expected to be able to write non-specialised text types such as letters, articles, reports and compositions for a given purpose and target reader, covering a range of topics. One of the tasks in Part 2 is based on an optional reading of one of five set books.

Candidates are required to carry out two tasks: a compulsory task in Part 1 and one task from a choice of four in Part 2. The word length of answers for each task is 120–180 words.

Paper 3   Use of English

Candidates are expected to demonstrate their knowledge and control of the language system by completing a number of tasks, some of which are based on specially written texts.

The paper contains five parts and 65 questions, which take the form of multiple-choice cloze, open cloze, 'key' word transformations, error correction and word formation task types.

Paper 4   Listening

Candidates are provided with short extracts and longer monologues, announcements, extracts from radio programmes, news, features, etc., at an intermediate level. They are expected to show understanding of detail and gist, and to deduce meaning.

The paper contains four parts and 30 questions. Each part contains a recorded text or texts and corresponding comprehension tasks.

Paper 5   Speaking

Candidates are examined in pairs by two examiners, one acting as **Interlocutor** and the other as **Assessor**. The four parts of the test are based on verbal prompts and visual stimuli and are designed to elicit a wide range of speaking skills and strategies from both candidates.

Accuracy of grammar and appropriacy of vocabulary, discourse management, pronunciation and interactive communication are assessed.

Marks

Each of the papers carries 40 marks after weighting.

Further information

FCE is held each year in March, June and December in 1,900 centres worldwide. Special arrangements are available for disabled candidates. These may include extra time, separate accommodation or equipment, Braille transcription, etc. Consult the UCLES Local Secretary in your area for more details.

Copies of the Regulations and details of entry procedure, current fees and further information about this and other Cambridge examinations can be obtained from the Local Secretary for UCLES examinations in your area, or from:

UCLES EFL
1 Hills Road
Cambridge
CB1 2EU
Telephone: +44 1223 553997
Fax: +44 1223 460278
e-mail: efl@ucles.org.uk
www.cambridge-efl.org.uk

In some areas this information can also be obtained from the British Council.

FCE content and marking

Paper 1   Reading

The FCE Reading paper contains four parts. Each part consists of a text and corresponding comprehension tasks. Part 4 may contain two or more shorter related texts. There is a total of 35 questions. The time allowed to select answers and record them on the answer sheet is one hour fifteen minutes.

Texts

The length of FCE texts varies from 350 words to 700 words, depending on the type of task. The total reading load for the paper is 1,900 to 2,300 words. The texts are intended to cover a range of recently published material and to appear authentic in form, presentation and content.

Texts may be of the following types:

- advertisements
- correspondence
- fiction
- informational material (brochures, guides, manuals)
- messages
- newspaper/magazine articles
- reports

Pictures and other diagrams are used where appropriate to illustrate the text; questions do not focus on visual elements. Some of the vocabulary may be simplified in the texts to keep it within the FCE level but such changes are kept to a minimum.

Test focus

The tasks in the Reading paper test candidates' ability to:

- understand gist and main ideas
- understand detail
- follow text structure
- deduce meaning
- select specific information

Tasks

There are 35 questions on the Reading paper. Each text is accompanied by a set of questions as follows:

Part	Task	Number of Questions	Task Format
1	Multiple matching	6 or 7	Candidates must match a heading or summary sentence to paragraphs of the text.
2	Multiple choice	7 or 8	Candidates must answer multiple-choice questions based on the text.
3	Gapped text	6 or 7	Candidates must select appropriate paragraphs or sentences that have been removed from the text and jumbled.
4	Multiple matching	13–15	Candidates must locate relevant information in the text or texts.

Multiple-choice and gapped-text questions follow the text; multiple-matching questions precede the text.

The language level of the instructions and individual questions is within the range of FCE.

Marks

Candidates record their answers by shading the correct lozenges on a separate answer sheet.

Two marks are given for each correct answer in **Parts 1, 2** and **3** and one mark is given for each correct answer in **Part 4**. The total score is then weighted to 40 marks for the whole of the Reading paper.

Marking

The Reading paper is directly scanned by computer.

Paper 2   Writing

The FCE Writing paper requires candidates to carry out two tasks; a compulsory task in **Part 1** and one from a choice of four questions in **Part 2**. Candidates are expected to write 120–180 words for each task, making a total overall word length of 240–360 words across the two tasks. The time allowed to complete the two tasks is one hour thirty minutes. There is an optional question on background reading texts in **Part 2**.

Test focus

Part 1 is a compulsory task in which candidates have to produce a transactional letter. Information is given about a specific situation through a combination of text and notes, sometimes supported by illustrations or diagrams. In **Part 2** there is a choice of four tasks from which candidates choose one. All of the questions specify why the piece is to be written and who the piece is to be written for.

    Parts 1 and **2** carry equal marks.

Tasks

In **Part 1**, the language of the reading input and rubric is well within the level expected of FCE candidates. Candidates are required to write a transactional letter in an appropriate style. The purpose of the letter and the addressee are clearly explained in the rubric. In order to complete the task successfully, candidates need to use the input provided in an appropriate way, expanding on the points given by using a range of structures and vocabulary.

In **Part 2**, candidates are expected to write one of the following:

- an article
- an informal/non-transactional letter
- a discursive composition
- a descriptive/narrative composition/short story
- a report
- a letter of application

There is an optional task (question 5) on background reading texts in **Part 2**. There are two alternatives in question 5 and candidates may select one of these based on their reading of the set texts. The list of set texts is published by UCLES in the Examination Regulations. Each text normally remains on the list for two years.

Assessment

An impression mark is awarded to each task; examiners use band descriptors similar to the ones on page 8 to assess how well the task has been realised.

    The **general impression mark scheme** is used in conjunction with a **task-specific mark scheme**, which focuses on criteria specific to each particular task, including relevance, length, omissions, range of structure/vocabulary, layout and register.

    Allowances are made for appropriate colloquialisms and American usage and spelling; marks are not specifically deducted for spelling errors, although a number of errors which interfere with communication will affect the assessment.

GENERAL MARK SCHEME

5	Full realisation of task set. • All content points included. • Wide range of structure and vocabulary within the task set. • Minimal errors, perhaps due to ambition; well-developed control of language. • Ideas effectively organised and paragraphed, with a variety of linking devices. • Register and format consistently appropriate to purpose and audience. Fully achieves the desired effect on the target reader.
4	Good realisation of the task set. • All major content points included: possibly one or two minor omissions. • Good range of structure and vocabulary within the task set. • Generally accurate, errors occur mainly when attempting more complex language. • Ideas clearly organised and paragraphed, with suitable linking devices. • Register and format on the whole appropriate to purpose and audience. Achieves the desired effect on the target reader.
3	Reasonable achievement of the task set. • All major content points included; some minor omissions. • Adequate range of structure and vocabulary, which fulfils the requirements of the task. • A number of errors may be present, but they do not impede communication. • Ideas adequately organised and paragraphed, with simple linking devices. • Reasonable, if not always successful attempt at register and format appropriate to purpose and audience. Achieves, on the whole, the desired effect on the target reader.
2	Task set attempted but not adequately achieved. • Some major content points inadequately covered or omitted, and/or some irrelevant material. • Limited range of structure and vocabulary. • A number of errors, which distract the reader and may obscure communication at times. • Ideas inadequately organised and paragraphed; linking devices rarely used. • Unsuccessful/inconsistent attempts at appropriate register and format. Message not clearly communicated to the target reader.
1	Poor attempt at task set. • Notable content omissions and/or considerable irrelevance, possibly due to misinterpretation of task set. • Narrow range of vocabulary and structure. • Frequent errors which obscure communication; little evidence of language control. • Lack of organisation, paragraph or linking devices. • Little or no awareness of appropriate register and format. Very negative effect on the target reader.
0	Achieves nothing: too little language for assessment (fewer than 50 words) or totally illegible.

All of these comments should be interpreted at FCE level, and referred to in conjunction with a task-specific mark scheme.

Marking

The panel of examiners is divided into small teams, each with a very experienced examiner as Team Leader. The Principal Examiner guides and monitors the marking process. This begins with a meeting of the Principal Examiner and the Team Leaders. This is held immediately after the examination and begins the process of establishing a common standard of assessment by the selection of sample scripts for all five questions in Paper 2. Sample scripts are chosen to demonstrate the range of responses and different levels of competence, and a **task-specific mark scheme** is finalised for each individual question on the paper. This summarises the **content, organisation, cohesion, range** of structures and vocabulary, **register, format** and **target reader** indicated in the tasks, in the form of satisfactory descriptors. The accuracy of language, including spelling and punctuation, is assessed on the **general impression scale** for all tasks. Markers discuss these individual mark schemes and refer to them regularly while they are working. A rigorous process of co-ordination and checking is carried out before and throughout the marking process.

Sample answers and examiner's comments: Book 3

The following pieces of writing have been selected from students' answers. The samples relate to tasks in Tests 1–4 of Student's Book 3. Explanatory notes have been added to show how the bands have been arrived at. The comments should be read in conjunction with the task-specific mark schemes included in the keys.

Sample A (Book 3, Test 1, Question 2 – Report)

> *You will find all kinds of shop in the college's area. First of all, there is a big supermarkt at only five minutes walk from the students' residence. It is open from 9. a. m to 7. p. m well furnished and not too expensive.*
>
> *If you don't like cooking, you'll have a large choice of pubs and restaurants, where you can have a good meal and meet nice people. Some of them could be too expensive for students, so you have to be careful and to read previously the menue. The White Horse is the oldest pub in the Town. It is always crowded and very noisy, but it is worth going there if you want to meet local people.*
>
> *You'll also find several bookshops in the town's centre. The shop assistants are usually very competent and helpful. Last but not least, a doctor's surgery, a chemist and a bank are located in Browning Street, not far away from the main building of the campus.*

Comments

Information is given about different kinds of shops (supermarket, bookshops, chemist) and relevant details such as opening times have been included. There is some digression on pubs and restaurants, which has brought the mark down from a Band 4.

The writing flows naturally and there is evidence of range. Relevant student vocabulary such as *residence, campus* has been included.

The piece is well controlled, with occasional non-impeding errors, e.g. *to read previously the menue*. Appropriate paragraphing has been attempted although perhaps not distinctly enough for a report.

The register is generally appropriate.

The target reader would be well-informed.

Band: 3

Sample B (Book 3, Test 1, Question 3 – Informal Letter)

Dear Susan,

How are you? I'm very well here in Rome. I'm here since the last week but I'm going to stay until the next week. Rome is precious, for me one of the most beautiful cities in the world.

   The museums and the archaeological excavations are magnificent. We have visited the Forum wich is all the monuments from the Roman period. The Coliseum near the Forum is beautiful and enormous (about 60.000 came here to see the lions vs christions fights), the Vatican city is beautiful. We saw the pope here in San Pedro. You will enjoy Rome because here the museums are very good. The Vatican museums are so big that we spend five hours for visiting it. The Borghese Gallery where the Apollo and Dague by Bernini is the Capitolium museum etc. Yesterday we went to S.Pietro in Vincoli, there is the Moses by Miguel Angel.

   Tomorrow we are going to the Piazza di Spaguna and to the Fontana de Trevi (where Anita Baker swim in the film "La Dolce Vita" by Fellinin.

   I will show you the photographs when I'll be back.

   Yours,

      Marianne

Comments

Plenty of detail is given on what the writer has done so far but there is very little about future plans and no reference to the group.

   There is evidence of range, with some good descriptive language used, e.g. ... *the archaeological excavations are magnificent.* A number of non-impeding errors are present, e.g. *I'm here since the last week ... The Vatican museums are so big that we spend five hours for visiting it.* At one point – *The Borghese Gallery ...* – there is lack of control.

   The letter is well organised, with some paragraphing and a good opening.

   The register is consistently informal.

   The target reader would find the description interesting but expect a wider range of information.

Band: 2

Sample C (Book 3, Test 1, Question 4 – Composition)

> "Violence in t.v. and on films can make young people behave badly."
>
> Many people belive that such kind of T.V and films are bad for young people. I agree with that.
>
> In my opinion is it is very easy to see such seans in there therefore they will be able to kow how to fight to other people and hurt to other people. However, the will not be able to know how it is hurt and dengerous is. It is so bad to grow up for young people that they might have alcohol and smoak, even though they are not grow up enough.
>
> To sum up. they should not watch such kind of programs until they have common.

Comments

Although the writer states agreement early in the composition, inadequate reasons are given. The script is also rather short.

There is little evidence of FCE level language, apart from some vocabulary items, e.g. *grow up, alcohol*.

There is serious lack of control and the errors made are basic, frequent and often impeding. The final sentence exemplifies this. The piece has been paragraphed and there is some attempt to use cohesive devices.

The register is acceptable.

The target reader would be confused and might not read to the end.

Band: 1

Sample D (Book 3, Test 2, Question 3 – Application)

Dear Mrs Robinson,

    I have read your advertisement in The Guardian Weekly's today issue and I am very interested in your job offer as a waitress I hope you will be interested in my application.

    First, I am a foreign student. French is my mother-tongue but I have also learnt English and German at school. Now I am learning English at the University to become a teacher in English for French pupils. My knowledge of French must be useful for you as the Eurostar attracks a lot of French visitors in Britain nowadays. As a student in English, I am both interested in earning money at summer time and in learning Britain and its inhabitants.

    Secondly, if I have no experience in working in a restaurant, I have already had a summer job in a shop. So, I am used to the wishes of customers, the concern in welcoming them clearly and the hurry in which you sometimes are. Then, I am 30 years old, that is old enough to understand choosy customers, but young enough to deal with hard work conditions and heavy schedules.

    To conclude, I am highly motivated to your job offer and free as soon as you need me. Looking forward to a positive answer,

    Your sincerely

    Betsy Prel

Comments

The points in the advertisement have been covered and the writer has submitted a strong application.

There is evidence of structural range and complex sentences are produced successfully. Very good vocabulary is also used, e.g. *conditions, schedules*. A few non-impeding errors e.g. *a student in English, learning Britain*.

Generally the letter is controlled and accurate; errors occur mainly when complex sentences are attempted, e.g. … *the concern in welcoming* …

The letter is very well organised and suitably paragraphed with an appropriate ending.

The register is consistently formal.

The target reader would consider the application seriously.

Band: 5

Sample E (Book 3, Test 2, Question 4 – Short Story)

> *Bernie woke suddenly and looked at the bed-side clock. It was three o'clock in the morning and he remembered it was his mother's birthday. So he thought to prepair a surprise and for when she woke up at nine o'clock everything must be ready. First of all he went to the kitchen to cook a chocolate cake, but he noticed there was no milk and it was imposible to do without it. So Bernie dressed up in silence and walked very slowly to the door. Obviously at that time in the morning everything was close and he thought in his friend Judith, she lived infront of his house but it was very early to knock to the door. So Bernie took some little stones and tryed to put them in her window. After a lot of time, Judith saw him and went to the door and gave him the milk. After that Bernie start doing every thing a little faster because there wasn't more time. He prepaired the cake and put a lot of balloons in all the house. At 8.30 he took a beautiful breakfast to his mother's room, everything was perfect, the cake had many candles on it and his mother was starting to wake up. Right on time!*

Comments

The writer has used the prompt well and written an imaginative story with a good ending.

A straightforward narrative using mainly the simple past. Some good vocabulary relevant to the story has been introduced, e.g. *balloons, candles.* There are a number of errors in structure, e.g. *he thought to prepair, to put them in her window.* Spelling is also problematic, e.g. *prepair, imposible.*

The story follows a logical sequence and linking devices are used to good effect. The final phrase: *Right on time!* is effective. Some paragraphing would have improved the presentation, particularly as it is rather long.

The register is satisfactory.

The target reader would probably enjoy the story.

Band: 3

Sample F (Book 3, Test 3, Question 1 – Formal Letter)

Dear Brecon Boating Holidays

We are 4 friends and we are interested in the cruise along the rivers and canals that you are advertising. There are some information that we want to know before making our reservations. First of all, we want to know how much it would cost us 1 week for four people. We also want to know how fast the boats travel and how far each day. Another thing that we think it is important is if we need to bring special clothes and if the cooking equipment is included or we also have to take it with us. Finally, we would like to know some more about loxury in your boats.

We are very happy and we really want to take part of this great and interesting adventure Please send us the answers of our questions and all the informatin that you think it is important and necessary to know.

Thank you,

Rona Storck

Comments

All the points have been covered.

A variety of indirect question forms are attempted. The opening sentence shows evidence of control. Some relevant vocabulary is used, e.g. *reservations*. Although there are some errors, these do not impede the meaning, e.g. *There are some information … how much it would cost us 1 week for four people … take part of*.

The letter is well organised: the writer makes early reference to the advertisement and states her queries clearly, using linking devices.

The register is occasionally rather informal for a letter of this kind, e.g. *We are very happy …*

The target reader would be able to respond to the letter and deal with the questions raised.

Band: 4

Sample G (Book 3, Test 4, Question 3 – Article)

Clothes and Personalities

Today, No one escape to the fashion. Even the ones that called themselves "alternatives" follow some "fashion" that belongs to them. We don't see people walking down the street wearing clothes from the '70s. We don't see either, 15 year old girls wearing clothes of people of 60 years old. We don't see people wearing scarf and gloves in summer. So, everyone follow the fashion: if distinguish us from other classes (middle class, low class, high class), from the other sex, from our parents, and from our sons. All these has an influence on our personalities: some people say that the way you dress reflect the way you are: Tidy, hard-working, if you care yourself, etc. Other people say that you dressed following the fashion, and you don't put your personal 'detail' on your cloth.

    Maybe, this thing of seeing "through" the cloth is an ability. The truth is that with or without this "ability", the fashion dictated what you are going to put next.

Comments

Although some attempt has been made at producing an article, the writer does not address the task adequately – a general description of trends is given, rather than own or friends' views. There is also very little on the link between clothes and personality.

There is some ambition, though this is marred by errors. Good vocabulary is used, e.g. *follow (the) fashion, distinguish, reflect, dictated.* However, these items are used inaccurately.

A high number of errors distract the reader. Communication is obscured at times, see e.g. sentence beginning *Maybe, this thing of seeing …*

There is some attempt to organise the piece, with a strong opening sentence. Paragraphing is insufficient and the article ends abruptly.

The register is satisfactory and article format has been attempted, including a title.

The target reader would be rather confused and would want more specific information.

Band: 2

Sample answers and examiner's comments: Book 4

The following pieces of writing have been selected from students' answers. The samples relate to tasks in Tests 1–4 of Student's Book 4. Explanatory notes have been added to show how the bands have been arrived at. The comments should be read in conjunction with the task-specific mark schemes included in the keys.

Sample A (Book 4, Test 1, Question 3 – Composition)

> I have seen a similar newspaper article, which said that there are a lot of children who don't go to school. Instead, they study in your house on your own.
>
> Why they give up? There are several reasons, for instance, bullied by other pupils or get bored.
>
> From what I have seen, there is no waste of time because if you want to have a nine–to–five job, they will ask you a general knowledge.
>
> When I went to a job interview three years ago, not only interviewed but they also tested my general knowledge after the interview without telling me in advance. I still remember this because I really regreted. I thought in my mind "I wish I had studied harder" at that moment.
>
> To sum up, anything you are being taught is not a waste of student's time. It will become your wide range of knowledge and invisible treasure. Moreover, thinking that is a waste of time is that you will waste your time.

Comments

Content
Some attempt to relate own experiences to the statement.

Accuracy
Omissions sometimes impede communication e.g. *not only interviewed*; *regreted*. Final sentence impenetrable!

Range
Patchy. Some good phrases e.g. *in advance*; *wide range of knowledge*; but poor control at sentence level means that they are not used effectively.

Organisation and cohesion
No clear development of the ideas – the division into paragraphs seems random.

Appropriacy of register and format
Impersonal *you* used inconsistently. Composition format attempted e.g. *To sum up . . .*

Target reader
Would be rather confused.

Band: 2

Sample B (Book 4, Test 1, Question 4 – Report)

Eating out in Berlin

Berlin is the capital of Germany. Because it is a large city there are so many possibilities where to go to eat or drink.

At first I would give you the advise to eat in the typical German restaurant "Four trees". It is in the centre of town situated. The food there is very delicious and it is suitable for your students to try German dishes especially at lunch–time.

About 10 km from the centre you can find the cafe "Rouge". In my opinion, it is the nicest one. The cafe is surrounded of a little park, where you could go for a walk afterwards. All cakes are home–made. My favourite cake is the strawberry–cheese–cake. Also the hot chocolate is tasteful.

In the evening it is the best to go to the bar "Moonlight". There you could try all the different kinds of German beer. If you don't like drinking beer you could try one kind of wine.

Of course there are not only German restaurants. My advise is to go to an Italian restaurant. The staff is very kind and polite. There you can eat pasta in many different kinds.

I've tried to describe you the best places to eat out and drink out and hope you will enjoy your visit.

Comments

Content
Content covers several places to eat and drink, with some reference to suitability for students.

Accuracy
A few errors especially spelling and prepositions, e.g. *My advise; in many different kinds; surrounded of a little park.*

Range
Vocabulary appropriate to the task e.g. *German dishes* and some clear, straightforward sentences.

Organisation and cohesion
Series of short paragraphs appropriate to an informal report; good conclusion.

Appropriacy of register and format
Consistent register, clear layout.

Target reader
Would have clear recommendations of where to eat/drink in Berlin.

Band: 4

Sample C (Book 4, Test 2, Question 2 – Letter)

Dear George,

I'm sorry I haven't written to you for so long. I was very busy with our cousin's Amanda wedding. It was a beautiful wedding.

As you know the date of the wedding was Saturday 21st of June. This Saturday morning, Amanda was very hapy because she was going to get married but sad because she was going to leave her father's house. Furthermore she was very anxious and all morning she was in frond of the mirror looking if she was prety.

The afternoon she put on her costum and we all went to the church. Amanda and Paul got married. The two of them were very beautiful and nice.

After the wedding we went to a tavern to celebrate it. Amanda and Paul took many wishes from the guests allover they took presents.

Uncle Peter took his daughter Amanda and Paul to dance. It was very funny because Paul didn't know to dance very well and his relatives too. The most funny thing in this celebration was that some of our aunts took some food for home. Moreover Melisa has a too short skirt.

The celebration finished at 2 o'clock in the early morning.

I'm looking forward to hearing from you soon.

Kisses,
Argyro

Comments

Content
No reference to cousin's absence but ample details of the wedding and guests.

Accuracy
Some awkwardness and a number of spelling errors.

Range
Adequate – some repetition of vocabulary; attempts at complex sentences partially successful e.g. *Furthermore she was very anxious and . . .*

Organisation and cohesion
Clear paragraphs and sequencing.

Appropriacy of register and format
Suitably informal tone and clear letter format.

Target reader
Would have an adequate picture of the day.

Band: 3

Sample D (Book 4, Test 2, Question 3 – Story)

> Dear reader,
>   As a child, I liked very much toys, some games, but also sports. Everyday, I was playing football with my friends in a small court and everyone was saying to me that I was a very good and strong player. Actually I liked hearing good words for me but I wanted something more exciting. So I told my father to join in a football team and my father agreed.
>   When I went there I saw some children playing football and other waiting like me. From the first time, I liked everything there. After I joined the team, the same day, I made new friends, footballers, and I began to play football with them. The master gave us, uniforms, athletic shoes, schocks and the uniform of the team: white shorts and green T-shirts. He also gave us a new ball, and suddenly he told us "Get ready, in a few minutes we are playing with paok, the opponent team". I was very enthusiastic, and my master gave me congratulations after the end of the match.
>   I will never forget my first day at the team.

Comments

Content
There is relevant narrative but it does not begin with the key sentence in the rubric. This brings a potential Band 3 mark down to Band 2.

Accuracy
A number of non-impeding errors e.g. *good words for me; and other waiting.*

Range
Some appropriate descriptive language e.g. *I was very enthusiastic; the uniform of the team; white shorts and green T-shirts.*

Organisation and cohesion
Suitable paragraphing and effective linking of the narrative.

Appropriacy of register and format
Opening inappropriate but layout is clear.

Target reader
Would probably ignore this piece of writing. Negative impact.

Band: 2

Sample E (Book 4, Test 3, Question 2 – Informal Letter)

Dear John

I'm writing to you about the former letter you have sent me and asked for me to give you information about my language becuase you want to lern it.

My language is an exelence language with many expresions. Never the les my language is very difficult. My language is based on our civilization. It's a beautiful language which it had give the base to other civilization and peoples to start a new life.

My language has a difficult grammar because it has many expresions and many word can be told with more over than one.

About how people speak this language I have to tell you that many words or expresions are not saying right.

If I don't answer in all your question send me another letter and aske me again. I will be very glad to have hearing from you again.

Your friend
Skremidai Andrew

Comments

Content
Little information or advice is given, and there is a degree of repetition. The second paragraph is in part irrelevant to the question set, and the final paragraph reinforces the impression that the task has not been fully addressed.

Accuracy
Poor structural errors leading to some loss of control e.g. *which it had give the base to, ... and many word can be told with more over than one, ... many words ... are not saying right.* Spelling is weak, e.g. *lern, exelence, expresions.*

Range
Inadequate. The structures and vocabulary employed are in the main simple, and attempts at more complex language are unsuccessful (see above examples).

Organisation and cohesion
Some attempt at organisation, but not successful. The letter is over-paragraphed, and ideas are not developed or worked into practical suggestions for learning a language.

Appropriacy of register and format
Inappropriate for an informal letter. The register used makes the letter sound rather distant, particularly in the opening and closing paragraphs.

Target reader
The letter would have a very negative effect on the target reader. The reader would have some indication of possible difficulties e.g. grammar, but no suggestions about how to start learning the language. The candidate does not actually mention which language is being described.

Band: 1

Sample F (Book 4, Test 4, Question 2 – Article)

It was a cold morning and a soft breeze was dancing in the air. We left the cottage by 8 am, after having had the most delicious English breakfast. DORKing, SURREY, is the most beautiful place in England at the early winter. The grass was wet, and we could smell the fresh air of the morning.

As we were going down to the village, the car suddenly stopped. Me and my friend Joana did not know what to do, as we were in the middle of the forest, in a foreign country, two hours away from the departure of our plain back to Portugal.

The car was rented, and we had to leave it at the airport. What should we do? We got desperate, and let me tell you that this was the most stressful day of my life. We walked and walked, all day long, neither with food or water, under the rain.

Finally we found a nice young couple, that was going to London. They were very nice and helpful, but the plain was lost and we had to sleep in heathrow.

I can assure you that rainy day was the most exciting adventure I have ever spent on holiday abroad.

Comments

Content
An unusual but acceptable interpretation of 'exciting'. A description of a full day is given.

Accuracy
Generally accurate but awkward phrasing in places e.g. . . . *neither with food or water, under the rain, . . . but the plain was lost.*

Range
Adequate for the task with some good relevant vocabulary e.g. *departure, airport, desperate, stressful, helpful.*

Organisation and cohesion
The opening paragraph does not seem to fit well with the rest of the narrative. Possibly an all-purpose narrative opening which the candidate has contrived to adapt to the question, though not wholly unsuccessfully.

Appropriacy of register and format
Appropriate for the task.

Target reader
Might query whether this day was exciting but would understand why it was special.

Band: 4

Sample G (Book 4, Test 4, Question 3 – Composition)

LIFE IS MUCH BETTER TODAY THAN IN THE PAST! THAT IS VERY REAL IN MY OPINION. I THINK NOW A DAYS THINGS ARE MUCH BETTER BECAUSE THERE ARE MUCH MORE ACTIVITIES TO DO, SUCH AS PLAY SPORTS, COMPUTER WORK, CINEMA ETC. TODAY YOU MAY TAKE SUPERIOR COURSES AS IN THE PAST YOU COULDN'T BECAUSE THERE WAS JUST NOT ENOUGH "BUILDINGS" FOR SCHOOLS AND PEOPLE WERE MUCH POOR, SPECIALLY IN SMALL TOWNS.
IN THE OLDEN DAYS THERE WERE NO CARS, NO TELEVISIONS AND NO MEANS OF GETTING INFORMATION SO PEOPLE DIDN'T HAVE AS MUCH KNOLEDGE AS THEY HAVE NOW. IN THESE DAYS WE HAVE ADVANCED TECHNICS AND SCHOOLS ALL OVER THE PLACE, SO THAT IS WHY WE ARE MORE CAPABLE OF GETTING SOMEWHERE IN LIFE THAN THOSE PEOPLE WHO LIVED IN THE PAST.
OVIOUSLY LIFE IS MUCH BETTER NOW, WE CAN GO TO DISCOS, TO THE BEACH AND ON THOSE CRUZES THROUGH THE WILD WATERS OF THE SEA IN MY OPINION THAT IS MARVALIOUS TO SPEND SOME TIME OF SO YES, LIFE IS MUCH BETTER NOW!

Comments

Content
The candidate agrees with the proposition and compares the past with the present with appropriate exemplification.

Accuracy
Very patchy. The candidate has problems with comparatives, e.g. *people were much poor*, but there are also some complex structures used successfully e.g. *In the olden days there were no cars ... and no means of getting information.*

Range
Limited range. An attempt is made to use relevant vocabulary, but it is not always successful, e.g. *technics, cruzes.*

Organisation and cohesion
The points could have been better organised. The ideas put forward do expand on the candidate's main argument, but the lack of discursive linkers e.g. *so; as a result; therefore,* makes the writing read more like a list of separate points. The concluding paragraph is weak.

Appropriacy of register and format
The register is appropriate for the task.

Target reader
Might be irritated by the presentation. It is acceptable to write in upper case as the candidate has done, but it is then essential to indicate clearly where paragraphs begin and end, which is not the case here. The reader would understand the points that the writer is trying to make.

Band: 3

Paper 3   Use of English

The FCE Use of English paper contains five parts. There is a total of 65 questions. The time allowed for completion of all five parts, including answer sheet completion, is one hour fifteen minutes.

Test focus

This paper tests the ability of candidates to apply their knowledge of the language system. **Parts 1** and **5** focus closely on vocabulary; **Part 4** emphasises grammar and **Parts 2** and **3** focus on both grammar and vocabulary.

Tasks

There are 65 questions in the Use of English paper. Each part of the paper contains a set of questions as follows:

Part 1

A cloze text of approximately 200 words, modified to place emphasis on lexical items, with 15 four-option multiple-choice items.

Part 2

An open cloze text of approximately 200 words, modified to place emphasis on structural words. The text contains 15 gaps to be completed by the candidate. There may be a small number of lexico-grammatical items.

Part 3

A set of ten sentences, each accompanied by a 'key' word and a gapped reformulation of the initial sentence. Candidates are required to complete the gapped sentence, using the key word, so that it has a similar meaning to the prompt sentence.

Part 4

A text of approximately 200 words which contains 15 lines (plus two example lines). Most lines contain errors. The errors are always extra and unnecessary words. Candidates are required to recognise the errors. No line contains more than one error.

Part 5

A text of approximately 150 words which contains ten gaps. Each gap corresponds to a word. The 'stems' of the missing words are given beside the text and must be transformed to provide the missing words.

Marks

One mark is given for each correct answer in **Parts 1, 2, 4** and **5**. For **Part 3**, candidates are awarded a mark of 2, 1 or 0 for each question according to the accuracy of their response. Correct spelling is required in Parts 2, 3 and 5. The total mark is subsequently weighted to 40.

Marking

Part 1 of the Use of English paper is directly scanned by computer. The other parts of the paper are marked under the supervision of a co-ordinating examiner. A mark scheme is drawn up in the light of pre-testing. This is adjusted at the beginning of the marking procedure to take account of actual candidate performance and then finalised. All scripts are double-marked. Question papers may be scrutinised during the marking if there is any doubt about candidate responses on the answer sheets.

Paper 4   Listening

The Listening paper is divided into four parts and is approximately 40 minutes in length. Each part contains a recorded text or texts and corresponding comprehension tasks. There is a total of 30 questions in the Listening paper. Each text is heard twice.

Recordings contain a variety of accents corresponding to standard variants of English native-speaker accent, and to English non-native speaker accents that approximate to the norms of native-speaker accents. Background sounds may be included before speaking begins, to provide contextual information.

The instructions which begin each section of the Listening paper are written and spoken. They give the general context for the input and explain the task.

Candidates are advised to write their answers on the question paper while listening. Five minutes are allowed at the end of the test for candidates to transfer their answers onto an answer sheet.

Texts

Different text types appropriate to the particular test focus are used in each part of the paper. They may be any of the following types:

Monologues:
- answerphone/freephone messages
- commentaries
- documentaries/features
- instructions
- lectures
- news
- public announcements
- publicity/advertisements
- reports
- speeches
- stories/anecdotes
- talks

Interacting speakers:
- chats
- conversations
- discussions
- interviews
- quizzes
- radio plays
- transactions

Part 1 consists of eight short, unrelated extracts of approximately 30 seconds which may be in the form of monologues or conversations. **Part 2** is a monologue or text involving interacting speakers and lasts approximately 3 minutes. **Part 3** consists of five short, related extracts of approximately 30 seconds each. They may be in the form of monologues or exchanges between interacting speakers. **Part 4** is also a monologue or text involving interacting speakers and lasts approximately 3 minutes.

Test focus

The tasks in the Listening paper test candidates' ability to:

Parts 1 and 3

Understand gist, main points, function, location, roles and relationships, mood, attitude, intention, feeling or opinion.

Parts 2 and 4

Understand gist, main points, detail or specific information, or deduce meaning.

Tasks

There are 30 questions on the Listening paper. Each listening text is accompanied by a set of questions as follows:

Part	Task	Number of questions
1	Multiple choice	8
2	Note-taking or blank-filling	10
3	Multiple matching	5
4	Selection from 2 or 3 possible answers	7

Task types include note-taking, form-filling, blank-filling or sentence completion for Part 2. In Part 4, questions may have two alternatives or three, e.g. multiple choice, multiple matching and true/false.

Marks

One mark is given for each correct answer. The total is weighted to give a mark out of 40 for the paper. Incorrect spelling is not penalised, provided that the candidate's intention is clear, except where a word has been spelt out letter-by-letter, for example, a proper name, and where this would actually be a test of the candidate's ability to follow the spelling.

For security reasons, several versions of the Listening paper are used at each administration of the examination. Before grading, the performance of the candidates in each of the versions is compared and marks adjusted to compensate for any imbalance in levels of difficulty.

Marking

Part 1 and **Part 3** of the Listening paper are directly scanned by computer. The other parts of the paper are marked under the supervision of a co-ordinating examiner. A mark scheme for each version of the Listening paper is drawn up in the light of pre-testing. This is adjusted at the beginning of the marking procedure to take account of actual candidate performance, and then finalised. All scripts are double-marked. Question papers may be scrutinised during the marking if there is any doubt about candidates' responses on the answer sheets.

Paper 5   Speaking Test

The FCE Speaking Test is conducted by two examiners (an Interlocutor who will conduct the test and speak to the candidates, and an Assessor who will just listen to the candidates) with pairs of candidates. The test takes fourteen minutes for each pair of candidates and is divided into four parts:

Part 1	Interview	(3 minutes)
Part 2	Individual long turn	(4 minutes)
Part 3	Two-way collaborative task	(3 minutes)
Part 4	Three-way discussion	(4 minutes)

A pair of colour photographs is provided for each candidate as the visual prompts for **Part 2**, together with a verbal rubric. The prompts for **Part 3** may be in the form of photographs, line drawings, diagrams, word prompts, etc., together with a verbal rubric. **Parts 1** and **4** do not require visual prompts.

Test focus

The tasks in the Speaking Test require candidates to interact in conversational English in a range of contexts. Candidates demonstrate their ability to do this through appropriate control of grammar and vocabulary, discourse management, pronunciation and interactive communication.

Tasks

The purpose of **Part 1** ('Interview': three minutes) is to test general interactional and social language.

In this part of the test, candidates respond to direct questions asked by the Interlocutor. Candidates are expected to expand on their responses, talking about present circumstances, past experiences and future plans.

The purpose of **Part 2** ('Individual long turn': one minute per candidate) is to elicit a sample of transactional language from each candidate.

In **Part 2** each candidate is given the opportunity to talk without interruption for one minute. Candidates demonstrate their ability to organise their language and ideas with an appropriate use of grammar and vocabulary. Each candidate gives information and expresses opinions through comparing and contrasting two colour photographs.

The purpose of **Part 3** ('Collaborative task': three minutes) is to elicit short transactional turns from each candidate by engaging both of them in the same problem-solving activity.

The tasks are designed to be open and speculative, and to give candidates the opportunity to demonstrate their range of language; the metalanguage of the exchange is as much part of the test as the utterances directly connected with the prompt. All **Part 3** tasks are shared; candidates are encouraged to talk together, without the Interlocutor, and should be able to express and justify their own views, invite the opinions and ideas of their partner and, where necessary or appropriate, negotiate a decision.

The purpose of **Part 4** ('Three-way discussion': four minutes) is to elicit a further sample of speech from the candidates by allowing them to participate in a wider discussion with the Interlocutor of the issues raised or touched on in **Part 3**.

At the end of the Speaking Test, candidates are thanked for attending but are given no indication of their level of achievement.

NB If there is an uneven number of candidates at a session, the last three candidates will be examined together.

Assessment

Throughout the Speaking Test candidates are assessed on their language skills, not their personality, intelligence or knowledge of the world. However, in order to be able to make a fair and accurate assessment of each candidate's performance, the examiners must be given an adequate sample of language to assess. Candidates must, therefore, be prepared to provide full answers to the questions asked by either the Interlocutor or the other candidate, and to speak clearly and audibly. While it is the responsibility of the Interlocutor, where necessary, to manage or direct the interaction, thus ensuring that both candidates are given an equal opportunity to speak, it is the responsibility of the candidates to maintain the interaction as much as possible. Candidates who take equal turns in the interchange will utilise to best effect the amount of time available and provide the examiners with an adequate amount of language to assess.

Marks are awarded throughout the test according to the following assessment criteria (four analytical marks provided by the Assessor, and one global mark provided by the Interlocutor) which together make up the candidate's linguistic profile:

- Grammar and Vocabulary
- Discourse management
- Pronunciation
- Interactive communication
- Global achievement

Grammar and Vocabulary refers to the accurate and appropriate use of syntactic forms and vocabulary in order to meet the task requirements at an appropriate speed of delivery.

Discourse Management refers to the ability to use an appropriate range of linguistic resources to organise sentences to form text. It embraces the concept of coherence, the use of cohesive devices and the appropriate complexity of utterances.

Pronunciation generally refers to the ability to produce comprehensible utterances to fulfil the task requirements. More specifically this refers to the production of individual sounds, appropriate linking of words, word stress, stress timing, the highlighting of words to indicate information or to enforce a message, and the use of contrasting pitch levels to convey the intended meaning.

NB At FCE level, it is recognised that candidates' pronunciation will be influenced by L1 features.

Interactive Communication refers to the ability to interact in the discourse by responding and initiating appropriately at the required speed and rhythm, in order to fulfil the task requirements.

The **Global Achievement** scale refers to the candidate's overall effectiveness in dealing with the four tasks in the test. The Interlocutor is required to give one global mark on this scale for the candidate's performance across all parts of the test.

Candidates are assessed on their own performance according to the established criteria and are not assessed in relation to each other. Assessment is based on performance in the whole test and is not related to performance in particular parts of the test. After initial training of examiners, standardisation of marking is maintained by both biannual examiner co-ordination sessions and by monitoring visits to Centres by Team Leaders. During co-ordination sessions, examiners watch and discuss sample tests recorded on video and then conduct practice Speaking Tests with volunteer candidates in order to establish a common standard of assessment. The sample tests on video are selected to demonstrate a range of task types and different levels of competence, and are pre-marked by a team of experienced examiners.

In many countries, Oral Examiners are assigned to teams, each of which is led by a Team Leader who may be responsible for approximately fifteen Oral Examiners. Team Leaders advise, support and monitor Oral Examiners as required.

The Team Leaders are responsible to a Senior Team Leader within their country, who is the professional representative of UCLES for the oral examinations. Senior Team Leaders are appointed by UCLES and attend an annual co-ordination and development session in the UK. Team Leaders are appointed by the Senior Team Leader in consultation with the local administration.

Grading and results

Grading takes place once all scripts have been returned to UCLES and marking is complete. This is approximately six weeks after the date of the examination. There are two main stages: grading and awards.

Grading

The five FCE papers total 200 marks after weighting. Each paper is weighted to 40 marks.

The overall grade boundaries (A, B, C, D and E) are set according to the following information:

- statistics on the candidature
- statistics on the overall candidate performance
- statistics on individual items, for those parts of the examination for which this is appropriate (Papers 1, 3 and 4)
- advice, based on the performance of candidates, and recommendations of examiners, where this is relevant (Papers 2 and 5)
- comparison with statistics from previous years' examination performance and candidature

A candidate's overall FCE grade is based on the total score gained by the candidate in all five papers. It is not necessary to achieve a satisfactory level in all five papers in order to pass the examination.

Awards

The Awarding Committee meets after the grade boundaries have been confirmed. It deals with all cases presented for special consideration, e.g. temporary disability, unsatisfactory examination conditions, suspected collusion, etc. The committee can decide to ask for scripts to be re-marked, to check results, to change grades, to withhold results, etc. Results may be withheld because of infringement of regulations or because further investigation is needed. Centres are notified if a candidate's results have been scrutinised by the Awarding Committee.

Results

Results are reported as three passing grades (A, B and C) and two failing grades (D and E). The minimum successful performance which a candidate typically requires in order to achieve a grade C corresponds to about 60% of the total marks. Statements of Results include a graphical display of the candidate's performance in each paper. These are shown against the scale **Exceptional –**

Good – Borderline – Weak and show the candidate's relative performance in each paper.

Statements of Results are issued through centres approximately two months after the examination has been taken.

Certificates are issued about six weeks after the issue of Statements of Results. Enquiries about results may be made through Local Secretaries, within a month of the issue of Statements of Results.

Paper 5 frameworks

Book 3 Test 1

Note: In the examination, there will be both an Assessor and an Interlocutor in the room.

The following rubrics use plural forms, where appropriate, although it is realised that a teacher may often be working with an individual student for practice sessions.

The visual material for **Test 1** appears on pages C1, C3 and C5 of Student's Book 3.

Part 1 (3 minutes)

Introductions
Interlocutor: Good morning (afternoon/evening). Could I have your mark sheets, please? Thank you.
My name is .... and this is my colleague ....
He/she is just going to be listening to us.
So, you are .... and ....? Thank you.
First of all we'd like to know something about you, so I'm going to ask you some questions about yourselves.

(Select one or more questions from each of the following categories as appropriate.)

Home Town
Interlocutor: Let's begin with your home town or village.
- Where are you from?
- Can you tell me something about (*candidate's town or village*)?
- What is there to do in the evenings in (*candidate's town or village*)?
- Which part of your town/village do you like most? Why?
- What kind of jobs do the people in your town/village do?

Family
Interlocutor: And what about your family?
- Do you have a large family or a small family?
- Can you tell me something about them?

Work/Study
Interlocutor: And what about you?
- Can you tell me something about yourself?
- Do you work or are you a student?
- What do you enjoy most about your work/studies?
- What qualifications did you need/will you need for your job/for the job you hope to do?

Leisure

Interlocutor: Now, let's move on to what you do in your spare time.

- Do you have any hobbies?
- How did you become interested in (*whatever hobby the candidate enjoys*)?
- Which do you prefer more, watching television or going to the cinema? What sort of programmes/films do you like to watch?
- What kind of sports are you and your friends interested in?
- What kind of music do you enjoy most?
- How do you usually spend your holidays?
- Is there anywhere you would particularly like to visit? Why?

Future Plans

Interlocutor: Now, thinking about the future.

- What do you hope to do in the next few years?
- How important is English for your future plans?
- What do you hope to be doing in five years' time?

Part 2 (4 minutes)

Interlocutor: Now, I'd like each of you to talk on your own for about a minute.

I'm going to give each of you two different photographs and I'd like you to talk about them. Candidate A, here are your two photographs. They show friends enjoying themselves in different places. Please let Candidate B have a look at them.

Indicate pictures 1A and 1B to Candidate A.

Candidate B, I'll give you your photographs in a minute.

Candidate A, I'd like you to compare and contrast these photographs saying where you like to go with your friends. Remember, you have only about a minute for this, so don't worry if I interrupt you. All right?

Candidate A: [*Approximately one minute.*]

Interlocutor: Thank you.

Candidate B, would you tell us which of these places you would prefer to be in, please?

Candidate B: [*Approximately twenty seconds.*]

Interlocutor: Thank you.

Now, Candidate B, here are your photographs. They show people reading different types of publications. Please let Candidate A have a look at them.

Indicate pictures 1C and 1D to Candidate B.

I'd like you to compare and contrast these photographs saying what sort of books or magazines you enjoy reading. Remember,

	Candidate B, you have only about a minute for this, so don't worry if I interrupt you.
Candidate B:	[*Approximately one minute.*]
Interlocutor:	Thank you.
	Candidate A, would you tell us what kind of books you prefer to read, please?
Candidate A:	[*Approximately twenty seconds.*]
Interlocutor:	Thank you.

Part 3 (3 minutes)

Interlocutor:	Now, I'd like you to do something together. I'm just going to listen.

1 E

I'd like you to imagine that your local council has decided to develop a piece of wasteland on the outskirts of this/your town and you have been asked for your opinion. Here are three of the plans that have been put forward.

Indicate picture 1E to the candidates.

Please talk to each other about how each of the suggestions might affect the local population, which group of people might benefit most from the development, and then try to reach an agreement about which suggestion would be best for the area.

All right?

You have only about three minutes for this, so, once again, don't worry if I stop you and please speak so that we can hear you.

Candidates A & B:	[*Approximately three minutes.*]
Interlocutor:	Thank you.

Part 4 (4 minutes)

Select any of the following questions as appropriate to encourage further discussion.

Interlocutor:	Which suggestion would be the least popular for the area in which you live?

Do you have any new developments in your area? If so, how successful are they?

How useful do you think it is to have supermarkets outside the city centre?

How important do you think it is to create wildlife parks?

What sort of leisure facilities are there in your area?

Thank you. That is the end of the test.

Book 3 Test 2

Note: In the examination, there will be both an Assessor and an Interlocutor in the room.

The following rubrics use plural forms, where appropriate, although it is realised that a teacher may often be working with an individual student for practice sessions.

The visual material for **Test 2** appears on pages C2, C4 and C6 of Student's Book 3.

Part 1 (3 minutes)

Introductions

Interlocutor: Good morning (afternoon/evening). Could I have your mark sheets, please? Thank you.
My name is .... and this is my colleague ....
He/she is just going to be listening to us.
So, you are .... and ....? Thank you.
First of all we'd like to know something about you, so I'm going to ask you some questions about yourselves.

(Select one or more questions from each of the following categories as appropriate.)

Home Town

Interlocutor: Let's begin with your home town or village.

- Where are you from?
- Can you tell me something about (*candidate's town or village*)?
- What is there to do in the evenings in (*candidate's town or village*)?
- Which part of your town/village do you like most? Why?
- What kind of jobs do the people in your town/village do?

Family

Interlocutor: And what about your family?

- Do you have a large family or a small family?
- Can you tell me something about them?

Work/Study

Interlocutor: And what about you?

- Can you tell me something about yourself?
- Do you work or are you a student?
- What do you enjoy most about your work/studies?
- What qualifications did you need/will you need for your job/for the job you hope to do?

Leisure

Interlocutor: Now, let's move on to what you do in your spare time.

- Do you have any hobbies?
- How did you become interested in (*whatever hobby the candidate enjoys*)?
- Which do you prefer more, watching television or going to the cinema? What sort of programmes/films do you like to watch?

- What kind of sports are you and your friends interested in?
- What kind of music do you enjoy most?
- How do you usually spend your holidays?
- Is there anywhere you would particularly like to visit? Why?

Future Plans

Interlocutor: Now, thinking about the future.

- What do you hope to do in the next few years?
- How important is English for your future plans?
- What do you hope to be doing in five years' time?

Part 2 (4 minutes)

Interlocutor: Now, I'd like each of you to talk on your own for about a minute.

I'm going to give each of you two different photographs and I'd like you to talk about them. Candidate A, here are your two photographs. They show different types of holidays. Please let Candidate B have a look at them.

Indicate pictures 2A and 2B to Candidate A.

Candidate B, I'll give you your photographs in a minute.

Candidate A, I'd like you to compare and contrast these photographs saying if you prefer active or relaxing holidays. Remember, you have only about a minute for this, so don't worry if I interrupt you. All right?

Candidate A: [*Approximately one minute.*]

Interlocutor: Thank you.

Candidate B, would you tell us which of these holidays you would prefer?

Candidate B: [*Approximately twenty seconds.*]

Interlocutor: Thank you.

Now, Candidate B, here are your photographs. They show children playing with different kinds of toys. Please let Candidate A have a look at them.

Indicate pictures 2C and 2D to Candidate B.

I'd like you to compare and contrast these photographs saying whether or not modern toys are better than traditional toys. Remember, Candidate B, you have only about a minute for this, so don't worry if I interrupt you.

Candidate B: [*Approximately one minute.*]

Interlocutor: Thank you.

36

Candidate A, would you tell us which of these toys you think is
better for children, please?

Candidate A: [*Approximately twenty seconds.*]

Interlocutor: Thank you.

Part 3 (3 minutes)

Interlocutor: Now, I'd like you to do something together. I'm just going to
listen.

I'd like you to imagine that a competition has been organised to
find the International Personality of the Year and you have been
asked to recommend a suitable winner. Here are some ideas of
the types of people who might win this award but you may have
other ideas of your own.

Indicate picture 2E to the candidates.

Talk together about which type of person is the most suitable to
win the award and then try to reach an agreement about who the
award should go to.

All right?

You have only about three minutes for this, so, once again, don't
worry if I stop you and please speak so that we can hear you.

Candidates A & B: [*Approximately three minutes.*]

Interlocutor: Thank you.

Part 4 (4 minutes)

*Select any of the following questions as appropriate to
encourage further discussion.*

Interlocutor: What is the most important quality for a human being to
possess? Why do you think this?

If you had to choose a personality from your local community,
who would it be? Why would you choose that person?

Would you like to be famous? Why/why not?

What do you think are the negative aspects of being famous?

Which person from the past do you admire most? Why?

Thank you. That is the end of the test.

Book 3 Test 3

Note: In the examination, there will be both an Assessor and an Interlocutor in the room.

The following rubrics use plural forms, where appropriate, although it is realised that a teacher may often be working with an individual student for practice sessions.

The visual material for **Test 3** appears on pages C7, C9 and C11 of Student's Book 3.

Part 1 (3 minutes)

Introductions

Interlocutor: Good morning (afternoon/evening). Could I have your mark sheets, please? Thank you.
My name is .... and this is my colleague ....
He/she is just going to be listening to us.
So, you are .... and ....? Thank you.
First of all we'd like to know something about you, so I'm going to ask you some questions about yourselves.

(*Select one or more questions from each of the following categories as appropriate.*)

Home Town

Interlocutor: Let's begin with your home town or village.

- Where are you from?
- Can you tell me something about (*candidate's town or village*)?
- What is there to do in the evenings in (*candidate's town or village*)?
- Which part of your town/village do you like most? Why?
- What kind of jobs do the people in your town/village do?

Family

Interlocutor: And what about your family?

- Do you have a large family or a small family?
- Can you tell me something about them?

Work/Study

Interlocutor: And what about you?

- Can you tell me something about yourself?
- Do you work or are you a student?
- What do you enjoy most about your work/studies?
- What qualifications did you need/will you need for your job/for the job you hope to do?

Leisure

Interlocutor: Now, let's move on to what you do in your spare time.

- Do you have any hobbies?
- How did you become interested in (*whatever hobby the candidate enjoys*)?
- Which do you prefer more, watching television or going to the cinema? What sort of programmes/films do you like to watch?

- What kind of sports are you and your friends interested in?
- What kind of music do you enjoy most?
- How do you usually spend your holidays?
- Is there anywhere you would particularly like to visit? Why?

Future Plans

Interlocutor: Now, thinking about the future.

- What do you hope to do in the next few years?
- How important is English for your future plans?
- What do you hope to be doing in five years' time?

Part 2 (4 minutes)

Interlocutor: Now, I'd like each of you to talk on your own for about a minute.

I'm going to give each of you two different photographs and I'd like you to talk about them. Candidate A, here are your two photographs. They show people doing different kinds of jobs. Please let Candidate B have a look at them.

Indicate pictures 3A and 3B to Candidate A.

Candidate B, I'll give you your photographs in a minute.

Candidate A, I'd like you to compare and contrast these photographs saying whether you (would) prefer to work indoors or out-of-doors. Remember, you have only about a minute for this, so don't worry if I interrupt you. All right?

Candidate A: [*Approximately one minute.*]

Interlocutor: Thank you.

Candidate B, would you tell us which of these jobs appeals to you more, please?

Candidate B: [*Approximately twenty seconds.*]

Interlocutor: Thank you.

Now, Candidate B, here are your photographs. They show different places where people live. Please let Candidate A have a look at them.

Indicate pictures 3C and 3D to Candidate B.

I'd like you to compare and contrast these photographs saying whether or not they are similar to the type of building you live in. Remember, Candidate B, you have only about a minute for this, so don't worry if I interrupt you.

Candidate B: [*Approximately one minute.*]

Interlocutor: Thank you.

39

Candidate A, would you tell us which of these buildings you would prefer to live in?

Candidate A: [*Approximately twenty seconds.*]

Interlocutor: Thank you.

Part 3 (3 minutes)

Interlocutor: Now, I'd like you to do something together. I'm just going to listen.

I'd like you to imagine that your local tourist office is producing five leaflets which will be used to give information about this area to visiting students and you have been asked for your opinion. Here are some ideas of things to include in the leaflets but you may have other ideas of your own.

Indicate picture 3E to the candidates.

Please talk to each other about the subjects that you think would interest students, try to reach an agreement about the five most important ones and then suggest how you could make the leaflets attractive.

All right?

You have only about three minutes for this, so, once again, don't worry if I stop you and please speak so that we can hear you.

Candidates A & B: [*Approximately three minutes.*]

Interlocutor: Thank you.

Part 4 (4 minutes)

Select any of the following questions as appropriate to encourage further discussion.

Interlocutor: What other ways are there of presenting information of this kind?

How important is it to include pictures in leaflets of this kind?

How easy is it to obtain information about your town/area?

If you need information about a town you want to visit, where do you go?

In what ways might a series of leaflets for retired people be different?

Thank you. That is the end of the test.

Book 3 Test 4

Note: In the examination, there will be both an Assessor and an Interlocutor in the room.

The following rubrics use plural forms, where appropriate, although it is realised that a teacher may often be working with an individual student for practice sessions.

The visual material for **Test 4** appears on pages C8, C10 and C12 of Student's Book 3.

Part 1 (3 minutes)

Introductions

Interlocutor: Good morning (afternoon/evening). Could I have your mark sheets, please? Thank you.
My name is .... and this is my colleague ....
He/she is just going to be listening to us.
So, you are .... and ....? Thank you.
First of all we'd like to know something about you, so I'm going to ask you some questions about yourselves.

(*Select one or more questions from each of the following categories as appropriate.*)

Home Town

Interlocutor: Let's begin with your home town or village.

- Where are you from?
- Can you tell me something about (*candidate's town or village*)?
- What is there to do in the evenings in (*candidate's town or village*)?
- Which part of your town/village do you like most? Why?
- What kind of jobs do the people in your town/village do?

Family

Interlocutor: And what about your family?

- Do you have a large family or a small family?
- Can you tell me something about them?

Work/Study

Interlocutor: And what about you?

- Can you tell me something about yourself?
- Do you work or are you a student?
- What do you enjoy most about your work/studies?
- What qualifications did you need/will you need for your job/for the job you hope to do?

Leisure

Interlocutor: Now, let's move on to what you do in your spare time.

- Do you have any hobbies?
- How did you become interested in (*whatever hobby the candidate enjoys*)?
- Which do you prefer more, watching television or going to the cinema? What sort of programmes/films do you like to watch?

- What kind of sports are you and your friends interested in?
- What kind of music do you enjoy most?
- How do you usually spend your holidays?
- Is there anywhere you would particularly like to visit? Why?

Future Plans

Interlocutor: Now, thinking about the future.
- What do you hope to do in the next few years?
- How important is English for your future plans?
- What do you hope to be doing in five years' time?

Part 2 (4 minutes)

Interlocutor: Now, I'd like each of you to talk on your own for about a minute.

I'm going to give each of you two different photographs and I'd like you to talk about them. Candidate A, here are your two photographs. They show people enjoying music in different ways. Please let Candidate B have a look at them.

Indicate pictures 4A and 4B to Candidate A.

Candidate B, I'll give you your photographs in a minute.

Candidate A, I'd like you to compare and contrast these photographs saying what sort of music you prefer to listen to. Remember, you have only about a minute for this, so don't worry if I interrupt you. All right?

Candidate A: [*Approximately one minute.*]

Interlocutor: Thank you.

Candidate B, would you tell us what kind of music you enjoy, please?

Candidate B: [*Approximately twenty seconds.*]

Interlocutor: Thank you.
Now, Candidate B, here are your photographs. They show people keeping fit in different ways. Please let Candidate A have a look at them.

Indicate pictures 4C and 4D to Candidate B.

I'd like you to compare and contrast these photographs saying what you do to keep healthy. Remember, Candidate B, you have only about a minute for this, so don't worry if I interrupt you.

Candidate B: [*Approximately one minute.*]

Interlocutor: Thank you.

Candidate A, would you tell us if you have ever taken part in activities like these, please?

Candidate A: [*Approximately twenty seconds.*]

Interlocutor: Thank you.

Part 3 (3 minutes)

Interlocutor: Now, I'd like you to do something together. I'm just going to listen.

I'd like you to imagine that a television company is going to produce a one-hour television programme about fashion and you have been asked to help plan the programme. Here are some ideas of things you might like to include but you may have other ideas of your own.

Indicate picture 4E to the candidates.

Talk together and try to reach an agreement about which four areas of fashion to include in the programme. Suggest which group or groups of people it might appeal to and say how you would plan the programme.

All right?

You have only about three minutes for this, so, once again, don't worry if I stop you and please speak so that we can hear you.

Candidates A & B: [*Approximately three minutes.*]

Interlocutor: Thank you.

Part 4 (4 minutes)

Select any of the following questions as appropriate to encourage further discussion.

Interlocutor: What sort of fashion programmes do you watch in your country?

What type of music is popular among young people in your country?

How much do you think young people are influenced by film stars/pop stars/fashion models?

What is the most fashionable thing to own among young people in your country nowadays? Why do you think it is so popular?

How have styles in make-up/hair changed in your country in the last five years?

Thank you. That is the end of the test.

Book 4 Test 1

Note: In the examination, there will be both an Assessor and an Interlocutor in the room.

The following rubrics use plural forms, where appropriate, although it is realised that a teacher may often be working with an individual student for practice sessions.

The visual material for **Test 1** appears on pages C1, C3 and C5 of Student's Book 4.

Part 1 (3 minutes)

Introductions

Interlocutor: Good morning (afternoon/evening). Could I have your mark sheets, please? Thank you.

My name is .... and this is my colleague .... He/she is just going to be listening to us.

So, you are .... and ....? Thank you. First of all we'd like to know something about you, so I'm going to ask you some questions about yourselves.

(Select one or more questions from each of the following categories as appropriate.)

Home Town

Interlocutor: Let's begin with your home town or village.

- Where are you from?
- Can you tell me something about (*candidate's town or village*)?
- What is there to do in the evenings in (*candidate's town or village*)?
- Which part of your town/village do you like most? Why?
- What kind of jobs do the people in your town/village do?

Family

Interlocutor: And what about your family?

- Do you have a large family or a small family?
- Can you tell me something about them?

Work/Study

Interlocutor: And what about you?

- Can you tell me something about yourself?
- Do you work or are you a student?
- What do you enjoy most about your work/studies?
- What qualifications did you need/will you need for your job/for the job you hope to do?

Leisure

Interlocutor: Now, let's move on to what you do in your spare time.

- Do you have any hobbies?
- How did you become interested in (*whatever hobby the candidate enjoys*)?
- Which do you prefer more, watching television or going to the cinema? What sort of programmes/films do you like to watch?
- What kind of sports are you and your friends interested in?
- What kind of music do you enjoy most?
- How do you usually spend your holidays?
- Is there anywhere you would particularly like to visit? Why?

Future Plans

Interlocutor: Now, thinking about the future.

- What do you hope to do in the next few years?
- How important is English for your future plans?
- What do you hope to be doing in five years' time?

Part 2 (4 minutes)

Interlocutor: Now, I'd like each of you to talk on your own for about a minute.

I'm going to give each of you two different photographs and I'd like you to talk about them. Candidate A, here are your two photographs. They show different places where people live. Please let Candidate B have a look at them.

Indicate pictures 1A and 1B to Candidate A.

Candidate B, I'll give you your photographs in a minute.

Candidate A, I'd like you to compare and contrast these photographs, saying what you think life is like in places like these. Remember, you have only about a minute for this, so don't worry if I interrupt you. All right?

Candidate A: [*Approximately one minute.*]

Interlocutor: Thank you.

Candidate B, in which of these places would you prefer to live?

Candidate B: [*Approximately twenty seconds.*]

Interlocutor: Thank you.

Now, Candidate B, here are your two photographs. They show animals with people in different situations. Please let Candidate A have a look at them.

Indicate pictures 1C and 1D to Candidate B.

45

I'd like you to compare and contrast these photographs, saying how you would feel in each of these situations. Remember, Candidate B, you have only about a minute for this, so don't worry if I interrupt you. All right?

Candidate B: [*Approximately one minute.*]

Interlocutor: Thank you.

Candidate A, in which situation would you prefer to be?

Candidate A: [*Approximately twenty seconds.*]

Interlocutor: Thank you.

Part 3 (3 minutes)

Interlocutor: Now, I'd like you to talk about something together for about three minutes. I'm just going to listen.

Here are some pictures of things we use every day.

Indicate picture 1E to the candidates.

Talk to each other about how important each one is in your life, and then choose three that are so important you could not live without them.

It is not necessary to agree with each other.

You have only three minutes for this, so once again, don't worry if I stop you and please speak so that we can hear you. All right?

Candidates A & B: [*Approximately three minutes.*]

Interlocutor: Thank you.

Part 4 (4 minutes)

Select any of the following questions as appropriate.

Interlocutor: What other things would you hate to be without?
How popular are 'fast foods' in your country?
How important is it to be punctual?
What is the most important piece of equipment or furniture in your home?
More and more people are travelling by car these days. How wise do you think this is?
What do you think life would be like without television, radio and newspapers?

Thank you. That is the end of the test.

Book 4 Test 2

Note: In the examination, there will be both an Assessor and an Interlocutor in the room.

The following rubrics use plural forms, where appropriate, although it is realised that a teacher may often be working with an individual student for practice sessions.

The visual material for **Test 2** appears on pages C2, C4 and C6 of Student's Book 4.

Part 1 (3 minutes)

Introductions
Interlocutor: Good morning (afternoon/evening). Could I have your mark sheets, please? Thank you.
My name is .... and this is my colleague ....
He/she is just going to be listening to us.
So, you are .... and ....? Thank you.
First of all we'd like to know something about you, so I'm going to ask you some questions about yourselves.

(Select one or more questions from each of the following categories as appropriate.)

Home Town
Interlocutor: Let's begin with your home town or village.

- Where are you from?
- Can you tell me something about (*candidate's town or village*)?
- What is there to do in the evenings in (*candidate's town or village*)?
- Which part of your town/village do you like most? Why?
- What kind of jobs do the people in your town/village do?

Family
Interlocutor: And what about your family?

- Do you have a large family or a small family?
- Can you tell me something about them?

Work/Study
Interlocutor: And what about you?

- Can you tell me something about yourself?
- Do you work or are you a student?
- What do you enjoy most about your work/studies?
- What qualifications did you need/will you need for your job/for the job you hope to do?

Leisure

Interlocutor: Now, let's move on to what you do in your spare time.

- Do you have any hobbies?
- How did you become interested in (*whatever hobby the candidate enjoys*)?
- Which do you prefer more, watching television or going to the cinema? What sort of programmes/films do you like to watch?
- What kind of sports are you and your friends interested in?
- What kind of music do you enjoy most?
- How do you usually spend your holidays?
- Is there anywhere you would particularly like to visit? Why?

Future Plans

Interlocutor: Now, thinking about the future.

- What do you hope to do in the next few years?
- How important is English for your future plans?
- What do you hope to be doing in five years' time?

Part 2 (4 minutes)

Interlocutor: Now, I'd like each of you to talk on your own for about a minute.

I'm going to give each of you two different photographs and I'd like you to talk about them. Candidate A, here are your two photographs. They show people enjoying a holiday by the sea. Please let Candidate B have a look at them.

Indicate pictures 2A and 2B to Candidate A.

Candidate B, I'll give you your photographs in a minute.

Candidate A, I'd like you to compare and contrast these photographs, saying what kind of holiday you would expect to have in each of these places. Remember, you have only about a minute for this, so don't worry if I interrupt you. All right?

Candidate A: [*Approximately one minute.*]

Interlocutor: Thank you.

Candidate B, which of these places would you prefer to visit?

Candidate B: [*Approximately twenty seconds.*]

Interlocutor: Thank you.

Now, Candidate B, here are your two photographs. They show different types of group photograph. Please let Candidate A have a look at them.

Indicate pictures 2C and 2D to Candidate B.

I'd like you to compare and contrast these photographs, saying whether you prefer formal or informal photographs and why. Remember, Candidate B, you have only about a minute for this, so don't worry if I interrupt you. All right?

Candidate B: [*Approximately one minute.*]

Interlocutor: Thank you.

Candidate A, which type of photograph do you prefer?

Candidate A: [*Approximately twenty seconds.*]

Interlocutor: Thank you.

Part 3 (3 minutes)

Interlocutor: Now, I'd like you to talk about something together for about three minutes. I'm just going to listen.

I'd like you to imagine that the local council wants to make people aware of the need to protect their local environment. Here are some of the things they would like people to think about.

Indicate picture 2E to the candidates.

Talk to each other and decide which three subjects are the most important, and then say how the council can make people aware of the problems.

You have only three minutes for this, so once again, don't worry if I stop you and please speak so that we can hear you. All right?

Candidates A & B: [*Approximately three minutes.*]

Interlocutor: Thank you.

Part 4 (4 minutes)

Select any of the following questions as appropriate.

Interlocutor: What do you do to protect the environment?
What is done to teach children about environmental problems in your country?
Who should be responsible for protecting the environment, individuals or the government?
Is it more important for governments to spend money on animals or people?
How interested in nature are you?

Thank you. That is the end of the test.

Book 4 Test 3

Note: In the examination, there will be both an Assessor and an Interlocutor in the room.

The following rubrics use plural forms, where appropriate, although it is realised that a teacher may often be working with an individual student for practice sessions.

The visual material for **Test 3** appears on pages C7, C9 and C11 of Student's Book 4.

Part 1 (3 minutes)

Introductions

Interlocutor: Good morning (afternoon/evening). Could I have your mark sheets, please? Thank you.
My name is .... and this is my colleague ....
He/she is just going to be listening to us.
So, you are .... and ....? Thank you.
First of all we'd like to know something about you, so I'm going to ask you some questions about yourselves.

(*Select one or more questions from each of the following categories as appropriate.*)

Home Town

Interlocutor: Let's begin with your home town or village.

- Where are you from?
- Can you tell me something about (*candidate's town or village*)?
- What is there to do in the evenings in (*candidate's town or village*)?
- Which part of your town/village do you like most? Why?
- What kind of jobs do the people in your town/village do?

Family

Interlocutor: And what about your family?

- Do you have a large family or a small family?
- Can you tell me something about them?

Work/Study

Interlocutor: And what about you?

- Can you tell me something about yourself?
- Do you work or are you a student?
- What do you enjoy most about your work/studies?
- What qualifications did you need/will you need for your job/for the job you hope to do?

Leisure

Interlocutor: Now, let's move on to what you do in your spare time.

- Do you have any hobbies?
- How did you become interested in (*whatever hobby the candidate enjoys*)?
- Which do you prefer more, watching television or going to the cinema? What sort of programmes/films do you like to watch?
- What kind of sports are you and your friends interested in?
- What kind of music do you enjoy most?
- How do you usually spend your holidays?
- Is there anywhere you would particularly like to visit? Why?

Future Plans

Interlocutor: Now, thinking about the future.

- What do you hope to do in the next few years?
- How important is English for your future plans?
- What do you hope to be doing in five years' time?

Part 2 (4 minutes)

Interlocutor: Now, I'd like each of you to talk on your own for about a minute.

I'm going to give each of you two different photographs and I'd like you to talk about them. Candidate A, here are your two photographs. They show people painting or drawing, in different situations. Please let Candidate B see them.

Indicate pictures 3A and 3B to Candidate A.

Candidate B, I'll give you your photographs in a minute.

Candidate A, I'd like you to compare and contrast these photographs, saying what kind of paintings you prefer. Remember, you have only about a minute for this, so don't worry if I interrupt you. All right?

Candidate A: [*Approximately one minute.*]

Interlocutor: Thank you.

Candidate B, do you ever buy paintings?

Candidate B: [*Approximately twenty seconds.*]

Interlocutor: Thank you.

Now, Candidate B, here are your two photographs. They show people taking exercise. Please let Candidate A have a look at them.

Indicate pictures 3C and 3D to Candidate B.

I'd like you, Candidate B, to compare and contrast these photographs, saying which type of exercise you think is best for keeping fit. Remember, you have only about a minute for this, so don't worry if I interrupt you. All right?

Candidate B: [*Approximately one minute.*]

Interlocutor: Thank you.

Candidate A, which of those activities would you prefer to do?

Candidate A: [*Approximately twenty seconds.*]

Interlocutor: Thank you.

Part 3 (3 minutes)

Interlocutor: Now, I'd like you to talk about something together for about three minutes. I'm just going to listen.

I'd like you to imagine that you are planning a seven-day tour of Britain.

Indicate picture 3E to the candidates.

Talk to each other and decide which of these suggestions would give an interesting and varied holiday, then decide which places you would like to visit and how long you would spend in each place.

It is not necessary to agree with each other.

You have only three minutes for this, so once again, don't worry if I stop you and please speak so that we can hear you. All right?

Candidates
A & B: [*Approximately three minutes.*]

Interlocutor: Thank you.

Part 4 (4 minutes)

Select any of the following questions as appropriate.

Interlocutor: What preparations would you make before going on a tour like this?
What are the most important things to take with you on a holiday like this?
Can you think of any problems with this kind of holiday?
What's the most interesting place you have ever visited?
Where would you most like to go if you had the opportunity?
Which towns in your country would you recommend a tourist to visit? Why?

Thank you. That is the end of the test.

Book 4 Test 4

Note: In the examination, there will be both an Assessor and an Interlocutor in the room.

The following rubrics use plural forms, where appropriate, although it is realised that a teacher may often be working with an individual student for practice sessions.

The visual material for **Test 4** appears on pages C8, C10 and C12 of Student's Book 4.

Part 1 (3 minutes)

Introductions

Interlocutor: Good morning (afternoon/evening). Could I have your mark sheets, please? Thank you.
My name is .... and this is my colleague ....
He/she is just going to be listening to us.
So, you are .... and ....? Thank you.
First of all we'd like to know something about you, so I'm going to ask you some questions about yourselves.

(*Select one or more questions from each of the following categories as appropriate.*)

Home Town

Interlocutor: Let's begin with your home town or village.

- Where are you from?
- Can you tell me something about (*candidate's town or village*)?
- What is there to do in the evenings in (*candidate's town or village*)?
- Which part of your town/village do you like most? Why?
- What kind of jobs do the people in your town/village do?

Family

Interlocutor: And what about your family?

- Do you have a large family or a small family?
- Can you tell me something about them?

Work/Study

Interlocutor: And what about you?

- Can you tell me something about yourself?
- Do you work or are you a student?
- What do you enjoy most about your work/studies?
- What qualifications did you need/will you need for your job/for the job you hope to do?

Leisure

Interlocutor: Now, let's move on to what you do in your spare time.

- Do you have any hobbies?
- How did you become interested in (*whatever hobby the candidate enjoys*)?
- Which do you prefer more, watching television or going to the cinema? What sort of programmes/films do you like to watch?
- What kind of sports are you and your friends interested in?
- What kind of music do you enjoy most?
- How do you usually spend your holidays?
- Is there anywhere you would particularly like to visit? Why?

Future Plans

Interlocutor: Now, thinking about the future.

- What do you hope to do in the next few years?
- How important is English for your future plans?
- What do you hope to be doing in five years' time?

Part 2 (4 minutes)

Interlocutor: Now, I'd like each of you to talk on your own for about a minute.

I'm going to give each of you two different photographs and I'd like you to talk about them. Candidate A, here are your two photographs. They show life in the city. Please let Candidate B see them.

Indicate pictures 4A and 4B to Candidate A.

Candidate B, I'll give you your photographs in a minute.

Candidate A, I'd like you to compare and contrast these photographs, saying what advantages and disadvantages of city life they show. Remember, you have only about a minute for this, so don't worry if I interrupt you. All right?

Candidate A: [*Approximately one minute.*]

Interlocutor: Thank you.

Candidate B, would you rather live in a city or in the countryside?

Candidate B: [*Approximately twenty seconds.*]

Interlocutor: Thank you.

Now, Candidate B, here are your two photographs. They show different kinds of entertainment. Please let Candidate A have a look at them.

Indicate pictures 4C and 4D to Candidate B.

I'd like you, Candidate B, to compare and contrast these photographs, saying why you think people enjoy watching entertainments like these. Remember, you have only about a minute for this, so don't worry if I interrupt you. All right?

Candidate B: [*Approximately one minute.*]

Interlocutor: Thank you.

Candidate A, was that the kind of entertainment you like?

Candidate A: [*Approximately twenty seconds.*]

Interlocutor: Thank you.

Part 3 (3 minutes)

Interlocutor: Now, I'd like you to talk about something together for about three minutes. I'm just going to listen.

I'd like you to imagine that you have been given this packet of greetings cards for special occasions.

Indicate picture 4E to the candidates.

Talk to each other about the different cards and then decide on what occasions you would send them, who you might send them to, and which one you like best.

It is not necessary to agree with each other.

You have only three minutes for this, so once again, don't worry if I stop you and please speak so that we can hear you. All right?

Candidates
A & B: [*Approximately three minutes.*]

Interlocutor: Thank you.

Part 4 (4 minutes)

Select any of the following questions as appropriate.

Interlocutor: When do you send greetings cards in your country?
On a special occasion, would you rather receive a card or a phone call? Why?
For a special occasion would you rather receive money or a present? Why?
How do you celebrate special occasions?
What kind of parties do you prefer, those with your friends or those with your family? Why?
Why do you think some people do not enjoy parties?

Thank you. That is the end of the test.

Book 3 Test 1 Key

Paper 1 Reading (1 hour 15 minutes)

Part 1
1 F   2 H   3 A   4 C   5 G   6 D   7 B

Part 2
8 C   9 A   10 B   11 D   12 A   13 B   14 C

Part 3
15 G   16 E   17 A   18 B   19 H   20 F   21 D

Part 4
22 B   23 A   24 D   25/26 B/C *(in any order)*   27 D   28 A
29 E   30 B   31 E   32 A   33 B   34 C   35 E

Paper 2 Writing (1 hour 30 minutes)

Task-specific mark schemes

Question 1
Content
Letter should enquire about disco availability for 9 July, giving times (8.30–12) and location (Ambrose Hotel). Mention of the number of people expected to attend (about 40). Questions about the cost and whether David Price can organise competitions for best dancers, etc. Should also specify the type of music wanted. Relevant additional information should be credited.

Organisation and cohesion
Clear paragraphing. Early reference to the disco. Ending suitable to a letter of request.

Register and format
Formal letter (though a more informal register would be acceptable if the letter began 'Dear David').

Range
Future tenses. Polite requests. Vocabulary to do with entertainment and parties.

Target reader
Would have a clear idea of the nature of the work and be able to respond.

Question 2 Report

Content
Report on the shops available locally in candidate's own town. Should include reference to more than one different type of shop and give useful factual information, such as what students can buy, quality of goods, opening times, etc.

Range
Language of description. Language of advice and suggestion. Possibly some personal opinion, though this should be subsidiary to the factual language. Vocabulary relevant to shops and shopping.

Organisation and cohesion
Clear paragraphs and possibly sub-headings.

Register and format
Informal or neutral (student readers); layout appropriate to a report.

Target reader
Would have enough details to know where to shop in the area.

Question 3 Informal letter

Content
Description of the people the writer is with, details of what he/she has done so far and some indication of plans for the coming week.

Range
Past and future tenses. Language of description. Phrases to convey enthusiasm (or lack of enthusiasm).

Organisation and cohesion
Clear flow and suitable paragraphing. Appropriate ending to an informal letter.

Register and format
Informal letter.

Target reader
Would be pleased to hear from the friend and have a detailed picture of what the holiday was like.

Question 4 Composition

Content
Personal opinions on the influence of violent films/TV on young people. Preferably some examples given, to illustrate the opinions.

Range
Phrases to introduce an argument or opinion. Adjectives describing violent/bad behaviour. Habitual present tense. Possibly some use of conditional tenses.

Organisation and cohesion
Clear paragraphing and some form of introduction. Effective use of linking devices. Each new idea in a separate paragraph. Strong conclusion.

Register and format
Neutral, conventional composition layout.

Target reader
Would have a clear picture of the writer's opinions.

Question 5 Background reading texts

(a)
Content
Two places to be named.
Explanation of choice.

Range
Language of description/summarising and explanation.

Organisation and cohesion
Linking of description, summary and explanation.

Appropriacy of register and format
Neutral: composition layout.

Target reader
Would understand why the writer thinks the chosen places are important to the book/story.

(b)
Content
Summary of development of story. Explanation of parts that are easy to follow and parts that are not.

Range
Language of summary, opinion and explanation.

Organisation and cohesion
Linking of summary opinion and explanation.

Appropriacy of register and format
The article should be more or less formal given the intended readership, but consistency is important.

Target reader
Would understand why the writer thinks some parts of the story are easy/difficult to follow.

Paper 3 Use of English (1 hour 15 minutes)

Part 1

1 A	2 D	3 A	4 B	5 B	6 C	7 A	8 D	9 A
10 B	11 B	12 C	13 A	14 C	15 A			

Part 2

16 this/that   17 in   18 to/for   19 but   20 date   21 be
22 not   23 make/be   24 what/everything/all   25 and
26 well/much   27 on/with   28 out   29 which/the (*allow* what)
30 most/more

Part 3

Award one mark for each correct section.
31 if/whether (1) we wanted/preferred/would prefer/like (1)
32 can't/don't we go (1) somewhere (1)
33 to avoid (1) queuing/having to queue/the/a/queue (1)
34 make a choice (1) between (1)
35 (he was) disappointed (1) he remained (1)
36 so crowded that (1) there was (1)
37 not cost (1) as/so much as (1)
38 did her homework (1) before watching (1)
39 have (1) run out of (1)
40 is/has been three years (1) since (1)

Part 4

41 of   42 more   43 ✓   44 ✓   45 ✓   46 herself   47 it   48 to
49 are   50 with   51 ✓   52 the   53 sure   54 us   55 ✓

Part 5

56 Chinese   57 communication(s)   58 reliable   59 births
60 unpleasant   61 death   62 warning(s)   63 commonly
64 religious   65 celebration(s)

Paper 4 Listening (40 minutes approximately)

Part 1

1 A   2 B   3 C   4 C   5 A   6 B   7 A   8 C

Part 2

9 Liverpool   10 1982   11 (Dr/Doctor) Jane Brown
12 five/5 glass houses/greenhouses
13 PITCHER(S) (*spelt correctly*) (plants/flowers)   14 cloud forest
15 fish   16 Wednesday(s) and Thursday(s)/Weds and Thurs (*both needed*)
17 Free/none/no (charge)   18 (a/the) banana tree

Part 3

19 D   20 C   21 B   22 F   23 A

Part 4

24 B   25 C   26 B   27 A   28 A   29 B   30 C

Transcript   *First Certificate Listening Test. Test One.*
Hello. I'm going to give you the instructions for this test. I'll introduce each part of the test and give you time to look at the questions. At the start of each piece you'll hear this sound.

tone

You'll hear each piece twice.

Remember, while you're listening, write your answers on the question paper. You'll have time at the end of the test to copy your answers onto the separate answer sheet.

The tape will now be stopped. Please ask any questions now, because you must not speak during the test.

[pause]

PART 1   *Now open your question paper and look at Part One.*
You'll hear people talking in eight different situations. For questions 1 to 8, choose the best answer, A, B or C.

Question 1   One
You hear the weather forecast on the radio. What is the weather going to be like today?
A getting brighter
B getting windier
C getting wetter

[pause]

tone

Weather forecaster: Good morning. Well, it's generally a cloudy start to the day with a little bit of rain in places, particularly in the north. But I think things will improve slowly as we go through the day. So, although staying cloudy for most of this morning, I think there's every chance of the sun coming through during the afternoon, especially in the south, and lifting the temperature to around 18 degrees, out of the light to moderate north to northeast wind. The north could turn rather cool this evening, but there is unlikely to be any further rain.

[pause]

tone

[The recording is repeated.]

[pause]

Question 2   Two
You are listening to a trailer for a radio programme later this evening. What is the programme about?
A music
B fashion
C films

[pause]

tone

Radio presenter: Tonight at ten tune into Pete Zimmerman's 'Night Moves', an irreverent look at the latest news from the West Coast shows … tonight Pete looks at the latest evening wear and celebrates the return of the coat and tie.

[pause]

tone

[The recording is repeated.]

[pause]

Question 3   *Three*
You hear a woman talking at a meeting about the environment. What is she doing when she speaks?
A issuing a warning
B suggesting a solution
C making a protest

[pause]

tone

Woman: The most shocking thing for me has been realising that we cannot any longer trust a carrot. I was always brought up to think a carrot was a healthy piece of food and I would happily just clean a carrot and give it to my kids without peeling it and I genuinely believed that I was doing them good. So when the government then turns round and says, 'Oh, sorry, we have a problem with pesticides and from now on we think it's safer to peel your carrots,' I decided something must be done about this and that's why I've come along to make my feelings known.

[pause]

tone

[The recording is repeated.]

[pause]

Question 4   *Four*
You hear a woman talking about her job. What is her present job?
A She trains people to use computers.
B She interviews people looking for jobs.
C She designs games to be played on computers.

[pause]

tone

Woman: I got into the industry completely by accident. I originally trained as a teacher but, after a few years of that, I got a bit fed up and gave it up. My degree had been in art and design and I actually went in to a job agency and they said, you know, 'What do you do?' and I said, 'Well, I teach and I draw in my free time' and then the next day they phoned me up saying, 'There's a small computer games firm, would you like to go for an interview?' So, I went along with no experience, having not drawn on computer or anything and I was given a manual and they said, you know, 'There you go, train yourself!'

[pause]

tone

[The recording is repeated.]

[pause]

Question 5 *Five*
You hear part of a radio programme in which listeners can take part in a competition. What is the prize?
A a book
B a film
C a map

[pause]

tone

Radio presenter: So, that's this week's competition. Now, the prize is this wonderful colour edition of 'Discovering Birds'. It's got excellent colour photography and drawings showing the natural habitat of each of the birds and very easy-to-understand diagrams and descriptions. It's small enough to carry round in your pocket and so even someone like me will be able to find and identify these birds in the field, and that's saying something, I can tell you.

[pause]

tone

[The recording is repeated.]

[pause]

Question 6 *Six*
Listen to this woman talking to her friend. What does she think of the new restaurant?
A It has good service.
B It has good food.
C It is good value for money.

[pause]

tone

Man: Hi Jane. Have you tried the new restaurant in town yet?
Woman: Yes, I went there last night with my mother.
Man: What did you think of it? I may be going this weekend.

Woman:	Well, it's a good job we weren't in a hurry because it took ages for the food to arrive. But when it finally did I have to say that it certainly was worth waiting for.
Man:	And what about the price?
Woman:	Well, it did cost rather more than we were expecting to pay. I think it'll be a while before we go back there.

[pause]

tone

[The recording is repeated.]

[pause]

Question 7   *Seven*
Listen to this man talking to his friend. Why is he talking to her?
A   to postpone a tennis game
B   to arrange a dinner party
C   to request some help

[pause]

tone

Man:	Hi Brigitte.
Woman:	Hi Dave. I hope you're not planning to cancel our game.
Man:	Ah. Well some friends of mine have just called and they're coming down to see me tomorrow. I haven't seen them for a while and – well – they've helped me a lot in the past. I'd like to return the favour by cooking dinner for them. It means I'll be busy tomorrow.
Woman:	Oh dear – that's a pity. I was looking forward to playing.
Man:	Well – what about the following day – same time?
Woman:	That's fine by me.
Man:	OK. See you then.

[pause]

tone

[The recording is repeated.]

[pause]

Question 8   *Eight*
Listen to this woman talking about an interview. How does she feel about it?
A   confident
B   annoyed
C   disappointed

[pause]

tone

Woman:	Well, I felt it was the right kind of job for me. I mean, I had the right qualifications and experience and I really thought I could do the job well. But – I don't know – they asked

me all the right questions but I think I was just too nervous. I seemed to be saying all the wrong things. I tried hard to make them want me but I could tell it just wasn't going very well. If only I could have a second chance.

[pause]

tone

[The recording is repeated.]

[pause]

That's the end of Part One.
Now turn to Part Two.

PART 2   *You'll hear a radio talk about a new educational and tourist attraction in the north of England. For questions 9 to 18, complete the notes which summarise what the speaker says.*

You now have forty-five seconds in which to look at Part Two.

[pause]

tone

Woman: Here we are today at the unique Saxon Bridge Rainforest Centre located near Liverpool. This is perhaps the last place you'd expect to find a tropical rainforest! Saxon Bridge was started in 1982 – so it's well-established now – by Dr Jane Brown who wanted to educate the British public about the problem of the world's most complex environment.

    She's created a whole forest in five glass houses. She started with just one thousand species but the forest now has ten times that number. The most striking are probably the beautiful passion flowers and a weird and wonderful plant called a – and you can't see them so I'll just spell that for you – a pitcher that's P-I-T-C-H-E-R – so named because they carry water like a small vase.

    Each of the five houses has its own specialist vegetation and climate: for example the first reproduces the conditions of lowland forest, while the fifth recreates the environment of the cloud forest. Many of the plants are in danger of extinction. Saxon Bridge's aim is to cultivate them so that they might be saved for future generations.

    Although the main base is plant life, the Centre also has a representation of birds, reptiles and small mammals including twenty species of small monkeys. The Centre aims to expand its wildlife to include fish. However, it should be emphasised that this is not a zoo. The real scientific focus is on the preservation of endangered plants. The animals are there because of the role they play in completing the forest system.

    If you're interested in visiting Saxon Bridge, you should note its special opening times. Because it's mainly an educational institution, certain days of the week are reserved especially for school parties and scientists: that's Mondays, Wednesdays and Thursdays. Saturdays, Sundays and Tuesdays are for the general public. Admission is free for school parties, children under three and wheelchair users. All others pay three pounds.

    Saxon Bridge is very easy to find from the motorway because there are plenty of large green signposts with the Centre's symbol – the banana tree – clearly visible.

[pause]

tone

Now you'll hear Part Two again.

[The recording is repeated.]

[pause]

That's the end of Part Two.
Now turn to Part Three.

PART 3   *You'll hear five different people talking about a drama group which they are members of. For questions 19 to 23, choose which of the statements A to F best summarises what each speaker is saying. Use the letters only once. There is one extra letter which you do not need to use.*

You now have thirty seconds in which to look at Part Three.

[pause]

tone

Speaker 1:   Well, I retired three years ago now and, at first I missed work terribly after twenty-six years, you know, I had nothing to do with myself, it affected me psychologically really. Anyway, I looked round and thought, 'I've got to start something fresh, do something differently'. And so I was looking through this booklet and I saw there was a drama group starting up locally and so I thought, 'I'll give it a try', I've always been a bit of a show off, you know.

[pause]

Speaker 2:   The way I see it, it's like a journey. There are five friends who do everything together. At the beginning one of us is missing, she's had an accident and we go to find her in hospital and see what's the matter with her, and anyway she disappears from there and we all get a bit worried and so set out on this journey to find her, and it sort of develops from there. It's not really like anything we've put on before actually, so there were one or two who needed convincing to go ahead with it.

[pause]

Speaker 3:   Very exciting. I mean when I first joined, I mean, I hadn't done anything at school, I'd never been to other groups or anything whatsoever. I came in because a friend said 'Oh, go on, come' and I thought, 'Well I'll go just once and see,' you know. I ended up being talked into taking the lead in the play that they were doing, never mind just joining the group. I was absolutely terrified, but I enjoyed it so much that I've continued ever since because, well, I mean, it is great fun.

[pause]

Speaker 4:   Well, it's not my first time on stage, that must have been when I was about thirteen, I was to sing in front of all my friends and, I'd had a few lessons, like, but I walked on to that stage and opened my mouth and nothing came out, I just dried up. I can laugh about it now, but it put me off for a good few years, I can tell you. These days, working with the group, I've learnt not to take any notice of the audience or anything like that because when you get to the age I am now people don't expect anything of you, so what you actually do is a pleasant surprise for them.

[pause]

Speaker 5:   I've been with this group four years. Umm, I've always done a lot of drama, you know, in different groups, just the usual sort of amateur thing, you know, but I happened to see an advert for this one and came along to give it a try. It was a new play they were doing and it was probably one of the greatest challenges I've faced so far because it was like nothing I'd ever done before and, you know, the people are very imaginative and open to new ideas and in that sense I couldn't wish for anything better.

[pause]

tone

Now you'll hear Part Three again.

[The recording is repeated.]

[pause]

That's the end of Part Three.
Now turn to Part Four.

PART 4   *You will hear an interview with a man who has just returned from travelling. For questions 24 to 30, choose the best answer, A, B or C.*

You now have one minute in which to look at Part Four.

[pause]

tone

Interviewer: Welcome to the programme. I have with me in the studio today, Steve Sedley, who's just returned from a rather unusual trip. Steve, how does it feel now you're back?

Steve: Absolutely marvellous … well, of course I had a wonderful time and I wouldn't have missed it for anything … but!

Interviewer: I'm sure everyone asks you this question but … what drives anyone to take time out from a successful career in banking to make such a journey?

Steve: Well … as a child I read a great many books about the explorers to the South Pole and the great travellers who crossed Europe and Asia … I wanted to follow in their footsteps in my own small way … Africa has always fascinated me so I decided to walk from south to north. The money I collected for charity made it worthwhile for other people but to be honest it was the fact that I had become disabled after a childhood illness and well … I just wanted to show the world what I, as a disabled person, could do.

Interviewer: Yes … indeed … well you certainly did that. How long was your journey in total?

Steve: Well … all in all it took two years and one month. It would have taken less time but I decided to stopover in one place for a few months.

Interviewer: Was that because you were sick?

Steve: I was only ill once on the whole trip and that was for one day … no, it was because I made friends with a guy I met on the road and he asked me to stay and work with his family to help bring in the harvest and the rest of the stuff around the farm … I really enjoyed the physical labour and the company of course … I was very reluctant to leave!

Interviewer: Yes … And how did your family feel about the trip?

Steve: Well, now they're quite proud and happy about it but I'm sure they'd be the first to admit that before I went they weren't sure what my motives were … here was this well-paid executive … loving his creature comforts … going into the bush.

Interviewer: What was the worst thing that happened to you?

Steve: Undoubtedly when I was suspected of smuggling – there was this officer at the border of … mentioning no names, who said unless I paid a fine he would hand me over to the police.

Interviewer: How did you get out of it?

Steve: Well … luckily there was a journalist from a respected local newspaper who saw the incident and threatened to expose the guy …

Interviewer: That was lucky …

Steve: It certainly was … it renewed my respect for the profession 'cos I used to have a very low opinion of the media … Actually, I can't get over how well my journey has been covered in the press … after all … lots of people do it … I can't see what's so special about my efforts.

Interviewer: One final question … would you do it all again?

Steve: Well, not exactly the same experience but I wouldn't mind trying it on a motorbike … now I'm getting older, it might be easier to handle!

Interviewer: Well, the best of luck to you with that. Thank you very much … Steve Sedley …

[pause]

tone

Now you'll hear Part Four again.

[The recording is repeated.]

[pause]

That is the end of Part Four.

There'll now be a pause of five minutes for you to copy your answers onto the separate answer sheet. I'll remind you when there is one minute left, so that you're sure to finish in time.

[pause]

You have one more minute left.

[pause]

That's the end of the test. Please stop now. Your supervisor will now collect all the question papers and answer sheets.
Goodbye.

Book 3 Test 2 Key

Paper 1 Reading (1 hour 15 minutes)

Part 1
1 E   2 C   3 G   4 D   5 A   6 F   7 H

Part 2
8 C   9 A   10 B   11 D   12 A   13 D   14 C

Part 3
15 F   16 A   17 H   18 G   19 D   20 C   21 B

Part 4
22 C   23 D   24 B   25 A   26/27 C/D *(in any order)*   28 D
29/30 A/E *(in any order)*   31 A   32 E   33 B   34 C   35 B

Paper 2 Writing (1 hour 30 minutes)

Task-specific mark schemes

Question 1
Content
The letter should give the friend clear details about the start of term, including registration, bookshop (and own offer), first lesson, party, adding relevant advice, credit given for additional relevant information/suggestions.

Organisation and cohesion
Suitable paragraphing, giving information in a clear sequence.

Register and format
Informal letter.

Range
Language of advice and suggestion. Vocabulary relating to learning English abroad.

Target reader
Would be pleased to hear from the friend, be fully informed and reassured about going on the course.

Question 2 Article
Content
Article should give writer's own opinions and advice about how to study successfully, covering the points in the rubric: study plans; good places to work in; exam preparation; making best use of leisure time.

Range
Language of opinion. Language of advice and suggestion. Possibly some conditional structures. Vocabulary relating to study and education.

Organisation and cohesion
Clear presentation of ideas. Summary conclusion, to underline own opinion.

Register and format
Semi-formal or informal, directed at new students. Article should attempt to engage the reader.

Target reader
Would gain good advice and be interested in the article.

Question 3 Application
Content
Application for waiter/waitress job should say why the candidate is right for the position, giving relevant background, about character, language(s) fitness.

Range
Personal description. Modal verbs. Vocabulary relating to work and catering.

Organisation and cohesion
Appropriate opening and closing formulae, with early reference to the advertisement. Logical presentation of information.

Register and format
Formal letter of application.

Target reader
Would consider the application seriously.

Question 4 Story
Content
Narrative, beginning or ending with the sentence given.

Range
Past tenses.

Organisation and cohesion
Link with the given sentence. Logical sequencing of the action. Story may only have minimal paragraphing.

Register and format
Neutral.

Target reader
Would find the story interesting.

Question 5 Background reading texts

(a)
Content
Brief summary of story. Statement of whether story will be popular or not, and explanation/justification of view.

Range
Language of summarising and explanation.

Organisation and cohesion
Linking of summary and explanation.

Appropriacy of register and format
Neutral; composition layout.

Target reader
Would understand why the writer thinks the story will or will not be popular in 100 years' time.

(b)
Content
Statement of which person in the book is most interesting to the writer. Description of the chosen person's character and an explanation of why the writer finds this person especially interesting.

Range
Language of description and explanation.

Organisation and cohesion
Linking of description and explanation.

Appropriacy of register and format
The article could be more or less formal given the intended readership, but consistency is important.
Article format, with clear opening and appropriate ending.

Target reader
Would understand why the writer thinks the person chosen is the most interesting character in the book.

Paper 3 Use of English (1 hour 15 minutes)

Part 1

| 1 A | 2 D | 3 B | 4 D | 5 C | 6 D | 7 C | 8 B |
| 9 A | 10 B | 11 A | 12 D | 13 B | 14 A | 15 C | |

Part 2

16 were	17 the/some	18 to	19 doing	20 his
21 great/good	22 in	23 had	24 be	25 for
26 that/which/and	27 by	28 an	29 few	30 of

Part 3

Award one mark for each correct section.
31 the end (1) of the course (1)
32 if you (1) aren't/are/'re not (1)
33 might/could/may be difficult (1) to find (1)
34 meals are included (1) in the (1)
35 there are (1) two reasons why (1)
36 accused Richard of (1) breaking/having broken (1)
37 can't/cannot (1) keep up/pace with (1)
38 me how (1) to get/I can get (1)
39 not as/so (1) well paid as (1)
40 don't/do not mind (1) which film (1)

Part 4

41 it   **42** too   **43** do   **44** the   **45** have   **46** ✓   **47** ✓
48 variety   **49** ✓   **50** so   **51** to   **52** up   **53** ✓
54 type   **55** who

Part 5

56 following   **57** drivers   **58** directions   **59** previously
60 failure   **61** manager   **62** unsatisfactory   **63** apologised
64 ambitious   **65** confident

Paper 4 Listening (40 minutes approximately)

Part 1
1 A   **2** B   **3** A   **4** C   **5** B   **6** C   **7** A   **8** B

Part 2
9 Paula (*not* Paul) JAKES (*spelt correctly*)   **10** History and Politics (*both needed*)
11 non-user   **12** (basic) word(-)processing (skills)   **13** speaking dictionary/ies
14 recorded newspapers   **15** (£)300 – (£)500   **16** Dr Stone   **17** 225431
18 radio (advert)

Part 3
19 F   **20** D   **21** B   **22** E   **23** A

Part 4
24 T   **25** F   **26** T   **27** T   **28** F   **29** F   **30** T

Transcript   *First Certificate Listening Test. Test Two.*
Hello. I'm going to give you the instructions for this test. I'll introduce each part of the test and give you time to look at the questions. At the start of each piece you'll hear this sound.

tone

You'll hear each piece twice.

Remember, while you're listening, write your answers on the question paper. You'll have time at the end of the test to copy your answers onto the separate answer sheet.

The tape will now be stopped. Please ask any questions now, because you must not speak during the test.

[pause]

PART 1 *Now open your question paper and look at Part One.*
You'll hear people talking in eight different situations. For questions 1 to 8, choose the best answer, A, B or C.

Question 1 One
You overhear two friends talking about going to a party. When is it?
A *tonight*
B *tomorrow night*
C *next week*

[pause]

tone

Woman:	You must come … Alan'll be really disappointed if you don't.
Man:	But I've got my exams all next week.
Woman:	But it only means missing one night's revision …
Man:	Well … how are we going to get there?
Woman:	My brother said I can borrow his car … as long as I get it back to him first thing tomorrow.
Man:	Oh, all right then.
Woman:	Great … I'll pick you up in half an hour then.

[pause]

tone

[The recording is repeated.]

[pause]

Question 2 Two
You overhear a customer talking to a saleswoman. What does he want to buy?
A *a shirt*
B *a suit*
C *a pair of trousers*

[pause]

tone

Saleswoman:	They're very nice, aren't they?
Man:	Oh, hello … yes … but I'm looking for something in navy blue.

Saleswoman:	Yes, sir. What size did you want?
Man:	I'm forty-two chest and thirty-two waist.
Saleswoman:	Right … well, actually we have a nice one in the window … if you'd like to try it.
Man:	Can I just try on the jacket … and then if I like it, I'll try the trousers as well.
Saleswoman:	Certainly sir.

[pause]

tone

[The recording is repeated.]

[pause]

Question 3   *Three*
Listen to this woman talking to her friend. What is her intention?
A to request
B to persuade
C to suggest

[pause]

tone

Jane:	Phil.
Phil:	Yes?
Jane:	Pass me the sugar, will you? I can't bear coffee without it.
Phil:	Sure. Here you are.
Jane:	Thanks.

[pause]

tone

[The recording is repeated.]

[pause]

Question 4   *Four*
Listen to this extract from a radio programme. What sort of programme is it?
A a weather forecast
B a travel show
C a sports programme

[pause]

tone

Cricket commentator:	Unfortunately, it's raining at the moment but we've been told that it'll definitely be fine and sunny tomorrow and we expect an exciting game. We're almost at the end of the tour – it's been a hectic few weeks, we've visited no less than five countries and played against some of the best teams in the world.

[pause]

tone

[The recording is repeated.]

[pause]

Question 5   *Five*
You hear a man telling a story about a colleague who had an accident. Where did the accident happen?
A   a sporting event
B   a music concert
C   a play at a theatre

[pause]

tone

Man: Well, I'd never seen anything like it. He must have used so much breath hitting that top note that he blacked out. The first we knew of it, there was a crash and he fell off the stage into the audience. One or two people ran over, but apart from a few bruises he was OK, and he got up and went back to his place, though he couldn't find his trumpet. And anyway, the incredible thing was that, through all this, no one stopped playing and the conductor didn't bat an eyelid!

[pause]

tone

[The recording is repeated.]

[pause]

Question 6   *Six*
You hear a radio advertisement. What is being advertised?
A   a disco
B   a social club
C   a means of transport

[pause]

tone

Announcer: It's the best ride you'll ever have! Jump aboard the party bus, the last word in party events. This is London's first nightclub tour, you get free entry into four discos in the same evening, and the fun continues on the bus as you travel from one to another. Ideal for birthdays, office parties or a night out with friends. For info and bookings call 881543. Group discounts available on request.

[pause]

tone

[The recording is repeated.]

[pause]

Question 7	*Seven*

You hear part of a programme about things to do in New York. What type of place is being described?
A *a museum*
B *a shop*
C *a factory*

[pause]

tone

Radio presenter:	New York has always been a centre of the fashion industry, its importance based around the development of practical styles for modern working life. The exhibition draws from the vast collection of clothes stored here, to provide a record of how New Yorkers have dressed themselves through the ages. The emphasis here, however, is towards the fantastic creations made for the city's social scene, as might be expected.

[pause]

tone

[The recording is repeated.]

[pause]

Question 8	*Eight*

Listen to this man talking to a taxi driver. Where is he going?
A *the airport*
B *the theatre*
C *the sports club*

[pause]

tone

Man:	Could you hurry please. I'm a little late. If I don't get there by twelve-thirty, they'll worry that I'm not going to turn up. They'll probably start without me and that'll cause all kinds of problems. It's the first play we've done for a long time, and everyone's nervous. We have to have a good run through the show to give us all some confidence.

[pause]

tone

[The recording is repeated.]

[pause]

That's the end of Part One.
Now turn to Part Two.

PART 2	*You'll hear a telephone conversation where a woman asks for information about different study aids for the blind. For questions 9 to 18, complete the Enquiries Record.*

You now have forty-five seconds in which to look at Part Two.

[pause]

tone

Man: Good morning, Banshire Blind Society, how can I help you?

Woman: Oh good morning. I'm ringing to make enquiries about equipment that might be useful for my studies. I've been blind for three years.

Man: Right.

Woman: … and I'm just starting a degree course and I wondered if you have any recommendations for equipment that might be useful.

Man: Yes, certainly madam … what we normally like to do is to take down some details and then we investigate what might be suitable and get back to you.

Woman: Yes, fine.

Man: Right. What's your name please?

Woman: It's Paula Jakes. I'll just spell that for you … J-A-K-E-S.

Man: Right and what's the course you'll be following?

Woman: History and Politics.

Man: History and Politics. OK. And can I just ask about your ability to use Braille? Would you say you were a very good user, a partial user or a non-user?

Woman: I haven't used it at all, I'm afraid.

Man: OK, that's no problem. I'll put down 'non-user'. That'll do. What about computers? Have you got any skills in that area?

Woman: I do have basic word-processing skills.

Man: Right, well that's certainly helpful. OK then, now did you have any particular types of equipment in mind?

Woman: Well … I don't know much about it but I was wondering about speaking dictionaries.

Man: Right … actually we have a lot of new stuff in that area.

Woman: And possibly recorded newspapers?

Man: OK. I'll put that down too. And what sort of price range were you thinking of?

Woman: Well, I thought around three hundred pounds to start with, but if I have to I'm pretty sure I could get a further two hundred pounds if necessary … so up to five hundred pounds really.

Man: Oh that's fine. There are one or two good products on the market in your range. Now … what I'll do is look through our files and talk to a couple of people and give you a call … What's your number?

Woman: Well I don't think you can contact me very easily during the day 'cos I'll be at college … I tell you what, could you call my tutor?

Man: Yes … sure … no problem, but I'd better have his name.

Woman: HER name actually. It's Dr Stone.

Man: Stone. That's fine … and the number?

Woman: OK, it's 225431.

Man: Fine, I've got that … right … I'll be getting the information to you in the next couple of days.

Woman: Thanks ever so much.

Man: Before you go, can I just check how you found out about our enquiry service?

Woman: Oh, yes. It was through the radio advert.

Man: OK, many thanks. Bye.

Woman: Bye.

[pause]

tone

Now you'll hear Part Two again.

[The recording is repeated.]

[pause]

That's the end of Part Two.
Now turn to Part Three.

PART 3 *You'll hear an advert for a travel insurance company where five people talk about bad experiences they've had whilst travelling. For questions 19 to 23, choose from the list A to F what each speaker is describing. Use the letters only once. There's one extra letter which you do not need to use.*

You now have thirty seconds in which to look at Part Three.

[pause]

tone

Speaker 1:   It was an old car but it had never broken down ... well except for the odd puncture or problem with the brakes ... but never when it mattered ... so anyway we were really upset when they took it and we had a lot of problems reporting it.

[pause]

Speaker 2:   My wife and I were on a driving holiday in Europe and we were walking along when suddenly we were surrounded by people. When they'd gone, I checked my pocket and somehow they'd managed to take it. It was such a pain spending days trying to get the right papers from the Embassy, and of course we couldn't move on until it was sorted out.

[pause]

Speaker 3:   We were driving up this really steep road and suddenly the engine just stopped for no reason and we were stuck. Luckily, of all things, a police car came past and they organised a pick-up truck and we managed to get down but it was really expensive.

[pause]

Speaker 4:   It was really hot and so ... stupidly we just left a crack in the window ... but that was enough and the whole lot was gone when we got back. Luckily we had all our important documents and wallets with us in the restaurant and we just had to buy some new things to wear and stuff but that was still pretty expensive.

[pause]

Speaker 5:   It was one of those things that really upset you 'cos you don't know exactly when and where it happened. At some stage I realised it had gone. Anyway, I didn't have any insurance so I just had to forget about it but I had to spend ages trying to contact my bank to send me out some more.

[pause]

tone

Now you'll hear Part Three again.

[The recording is repeated.]

[pause]

That is the end of Part Three.
Now turn to Part Four.

PART 4 *You'll hear part of a radio programme about a problem caused by birds in a seaside town. For questions 24 to 30, decide whether the statements are TRUE or FALSE. Write T for True or F for False.*

You now have one minute in which to look at Part Four.

[pause]

tone

Interviewer:	A seaside town is at war with a part of its population. The attackers are sea birds who have got a taste for fast food. Anything, in fact, they can get from the tourists enjoying an open-air lunch on the seafront. I spoke to some people who'd been attacked.
Tourist:	My husband had just got me a burger, and I'd had one bite out of it, and a bird came right up close and whipped it away from me, from my hand. And then there was a little boy, they'd just got him some fish and chips and that, and the bird came and whipped it all away, the whole tray, and the poor little kid, I felt so sorry for him, because it was a horrible experience, even for me, you know.
Interviewer:	All around the harbour here, you'll hear the same stories. The Town Council have been trying to do something about the problem, Malcolm Vale is the Town Clerk and he's with me now. So is Jenny Samson, an expert on sea birds. Malcolm, hasn't this always been a problem?
Malcolm:	Unfortunately, it's a problem that's developed over a long time. Once upon a time the birds were encouraged by fishermen to come in and clean their nets. The town has always been a source of food for them; they steal from rubbish bins, some people used to feed them.
Interviewer:	What action have you taken?
Malcolm:	We've had signs put up asking the public not to feed them. The more people that feed them, the more birds we're going to have and the more this will become a way of life for them. We've got the rubbish bins securely covered to deny that as a food source.
Interviewer:	Is that going to make any difference, Jenny?
Jenny:	Well, the intention's good, but unfortunately if you take away the birds' source of food that may make them more aggressive and certainly it appears that they are getting more desperate to get hold of food, and that's what we are seeing now.
Interviewer:	So, Malcolm, is there another solution?
Malcolm:	Well, we borrowed an electronic system from an airport which is meant to keep birds away. Just to see if it would work, because they're expensive to buy. And when we first started using it, it was extremely effective, but to a certain extent I think their need for food is probably greater than their sense of danger, because they soon got used to it, and seemed not to take much notice.
Interviewer:	Jenny, do you have a solution?
Jenny:	Yes, egg pricking can reduce the number of birds.
Interviewer:	How does that work?

Jenny: Well, if you prick the eggs, the young will not develop, the young will not be born. It's better to do that than taking the eggs away because that only makes the parent birds lay more eggs.

Interviewer: Malcolm, have you tried this egg pricking?

Malcolm: Oh yes, but remember these birds can live for up to 32 years, so that's a long-term measure. We need something that's going to help us now. It's a very difficult question. We are watching the situation again this summer and we'll be discussing it again, but we may have to find a more direct method of reducing numbers.

[pause]

tone

Now you'll hear Part Four again.

[The recording is repeated.]

[pause]

That is the end of Part Four.

There'll now be a pause of five minutes for you to copy your answers onto the separate answer sheet. I'll remind you when there's one minute left, so that you're sure to finish in time.

[pause]

You have one more minute left.

[pause]

That's the end of the test. Please stop now. Your supervisor will now collect all the question papers and answer sheets.
Goodbye.

Book 3 Test 3 Key

Paper 1 **Reading** (1 hour 15 minutes)

Part 1

1 C   2 F   3 D   4 B   5 A   6 E

Part 2

7 C   8 A   9 A   10 B   11 D   12 A   13 C   14 A

Part 3

15 D   16 G   17 B   18 A   19 F   20 E

Part 4

21 E   22 D   23 A   24 A   25 C   26 E   27 C
28 B   29 A   30 C   31 A   32 D   33 B   34 C   35 E

Paper 2 **Writing** (1 hour 30 minutes)

Task-specific mark schemes

Question 1

Content
Request for information about the boating holidays, asking about the standard of the boats/meaning of 'luxury'; the cost (4 people for 1 week); the distance travelled per day; the cooking equipment provided; any special clothes needed. Relevant additional information should be credited.

Organisation and cohesion
Early reference to the advertisement. Concise description of requirements. Suitable ending.

Register and format
Formal letter.

Range
Phrases to request information. Variety of question forms. Vocabulary relating to boats and holidays.

Target reader
Would have a clear picture of writer's requirements and be able to respond.

Question 2   Story

Content
Narrative, beginning or ending with the sentence given.

Range
Past tenses. Some phrases to describe emotions.

Organisation and cohesion
Link with the given sentence. Story may only have minimal paragraphing.

Register and format
Neutral.

Target reader
Would be interested in the story.

Question 3   Article

Content
Information on the sporting event, which could be something like a tennis tournament or a sports day with different kinds of matches. Should give details of the college's results and what the event was like. Could include facts such as final scores, names of key players, etc. Some reference to the unexpected success.

Range
Past tenses. Factual and descriptive language. Sporting vocabulary.

Organisation and cohesion
Title desirable. Clear paragraphing.

Register and format
Neutral/Informal (article written for the college newspaper).

Target reader
Would be interested and informed.

Question 4   Report

Content
Report should give details of the recent group tour escorting elderly visitors around important buildings, commenting on aspects such as transport, facilities, timing, etc., as well as giving recommendations for similar future tours.

Range
Language of description. Language of suggestion/recommendation. Possibly some personal opinion, though this should be subsidiary to the factual language.

Organisation and cohesion
Clear paragraphs; sub-headings a possibility but not essential.

Register and format
Formal, layout appropriate to a report.

Target reader
Would be informed about the tour and be able to plan future tours.

Question 5 *Background reading texts*

(a)
Content
Favourite character and actor/actress to be named.
Explanation of choice.

Range
Language of description/summarising and explanation.

Organisation and cohesion
Linking of description/summary and explanation.

Appropriacy of register and format
Neutral; composition layout.

Target reader
Would understand why the writer thinks the chosen actor/actress could play the character chosen.

(b)
Content
Statement and brief summary of events/situations the writer believes could or could not happen in their country nowadays. Explanation of why/why not.

Range
Language of summarising, opinion, and explanation.

Organisation and cohesion
Linking of summary, opinion, and explanation.

Appropriacy of register and format
Neutral; composition layout.

Target reader
Would understand why the writer thinks these events/situations could or could not occur in their country nowadays.

Paper 3 Use of English (1 hour 15 minutes)

Part 1

1 B	2 A	3 C	4 B	5 C	6 A	7 D	8 A	9 C
10 C	11 A	12 A	13 D	14 B	15 A			

Part 2

16 from	17 which/that	18 had/needed	19 the	20 out
21 took	22 made	23 that	24 off/out	25 have
26 and	27 what	28 were	29 There	30 been

Part 3

Award one mark for each correct section.
31 went/got/travelled to Liverpool (1) by train (1)
32 without (1) thanking us for our (1)
33 for/(that) there/it will be/to have (1) better (1)
34 's/is responsible (1) for locking (1)
35 had been/was successful (1) in/at giving (1)
36 fell/was asleep (1) as soon/just (1)
37 probably won't/will not (1) see each (1)
38 looking forward to (1) seeing you (1)
39 (can) still remember/recall (1) every/each (1)
40 caused us to (1) get (1)

Part 4

41 that	42 ✓	43 kind	44 ✓	45 done	46 it
47 one	48 them	49 ✓	50 so	51 ✓	52 much
53 the	54 ✓	55 in			

Part 5

56 originally   57 fighters   58 violence   59 respectful
60 inexpensive   61 youngsters   62 instructors   63 demanding
64 strength   65 enjoyable

Paper 4 Listening (40 minutes approximately)

Part 1
1 B   2 A   3 B   4 B   5 A   6 A   7 C   8 C

Part 2
9 used/second(-)hand   10 (their) money back
11 (they) don't like them/are not/aren't satisfied/unsatisfied
12 electrical (goods)   13 washing machine   14 (someone else's/a) sock
15 display model   16 documents/guarantee/instructions
17 box(es) (not new or)   18 ask (lots of/a lot of) questions

Part 3
19 C   20 F   21 E   22 A   23 D

Part 4
24 T   25 F   26 F   27 T   28 F   29 T   30 F

Transcript   *First Certificate Listening Test. Test Three.*
Hello. I'm going to give you the instructions for this test. I'll introduce each part of the test and give you time to look at the questions. At the start of each piece you'll hear this sound.

tone

You'll hear each piece twice.

Remember, while you're listening, write your answers on the question paper. You'll have time at the end of the test to copy your answers onto the separate answer sheet.

The tape will now be stopped. Please ask any questions now, because you must not speak during the test.

[pause]

PART 1 *Now open your question paper and look at Part One.*
You'll hear people talking in eight different situations. For questions 1 to 8, choose the best answer, A, B or C.

Question 1 One
Listen to this girl talking about her new boss. How did she feel after she met him?
A delighted
B disappointed
C relieved

[pause]

tone

Girl: So there I was in my best clothes, arrived extra early to make a good impression and guess what? When he turned up I recognised him – yes, we were at school together. The only thing is I couldn't stand him then, he was awful and I bet he hasn't changed. It's going to be really dreadful working under him. I was so looking forward to having a new boss as well.

[pause]

tone

[The recording is repeated.]

[pause]

Question 2 Two
You overhear two friends talking about a birthday present one of them has just received. What is it?
A a television
B a cassette player
C a computer

[pause]

tone

Boy 1: It was a real shock 'cos I hadn't expected anything nearly so expensive!
Boy 2: Lucky you! Where are you going to put it?
Boy 1: Well, I thought in the study.

Boy 2: Why not in your room?
Boy 1: Well, the reception's quite bad on that side, you get a much better picture at the front.
Boy 2: Won't it be noisy for your Mum and Dad?
Boy 1: Oh … they won't mind!

[pause]

tone

[The recording is repeated.]

[pause]

Question 3   *Three*
You overhear two friends talking about a garden party they attended. What was the problem?
A the people
B the weather
C the place

[pause]

tone

Woman 1: It was pretty awful, wasn't it?
Woman 2: I know, and it's such a pity because we were all really looking forward to it.
Woman 1: When everyone had to come rushing in absolutely soaking wet I couldn't believe it!
Woman 2: It came down so quickly and it had been such a lovely bright morning.
Woman 1: And that amazing place, the garden and the lovely bright marquee.
Woman 2: Her family were furious. All that money.

[pause]

tone

[The recording is repeated.]

[pause]

Question 4   *Four*
On a visit to a college, you overhear part of a lesson. What is the subject of the lesson?
A health and safety
B child development
C food preparation

[pause]

tone

Woman: When you're very young, eating is a hands-on experience. Food is not just a matter of taste and smell, it's feel too. Babies learn by feeling things. It's a way of double-checking on what their eyes can see. So, next time your baby sister splatters you with her dinner, remember it's all part of the learning experience.

[pause]

tone

[The recording is repeated.]

[pause]

Question 5   *Five*
Listen to this critic talking about a film. What sort of film is it?
A *a comedy*
B *a romance*
C *a thriller*

[pause]

tone

Critic: Well, I have to say I thoroughly enjoyed this film. I'm sure it'll be a box office hit this
summer. Watch out for Roland Bernz, better known for his roles in action packed
adventures, chasing the girls, he's really convincing in his first attempt as a funny man –
lots of good lines had the audience laughing to the end.

[pause]

tone

[The recording is repeated.]

[pause]

Question 6   *Six*
*Listen to this boy talking to a friend about flying. How does he feel about
flying?*
A *excited*
B *depressed*
C *scared*

[pause]

tone

Girl: Hi Paul – looking forward to your holiday?
Boy: Oh, yeah – it's going to be great. Though I'm a bit worried that I've packed the wrong
clothes. I don't think the weather's going to be as good as I hoped.
Girl: You're flying on Saturday, aren't you?
Boy: That's right – my first flight.
Girl: I was terrified the first time I went in an aeroplane.
Boy: Oh, I can't wait. I bet it'll be the highlight of the trip. I'm only sad that you're not coming
with me.
Girl: Maybe next time, Paul.

[pause]

tone

[The recording is repeated.]

[pause]

Question 7 *Seven*
You hear an artist talking about her work. What type of artist is she?
A a photographer
B a sculptor
C a painter

[pause]

tone

Artist: You have to make a person look as if they're alive. You can look at a piece of sculpture and it's very lifelike and has a presence in itself, it already has depth; a picture you have to create from a flat surface. In photography, you know you're always going to get an image anyway. But when I start, I don't even know whether I'm going to manage it. You start off with a white canvas and a tray of paints in front of you and that's all.

[pause]

tone

[The recording is repeated.]

[pause]

Question 8 *Eight*
Listen to this woman leaving a phone message. Why is she phoning?
A She is complaining about something.
B She is requesting something.
C She is apologising about something.

[pause]

tone

Man: This is Dave Edmonds' answerphone. I'm not at home at the moment. Please leave a message after the tone. (beeeeeep)
Woman: Dave, this is Janet. I just remembered that you'd asked me to book a table at the Italian restaurant this evening. I've left it a bit late I'm afraid. I hope you're not going to be too angry. I've just phoned them and they're booked up. I know it's your favourite place. I'm not sure what to do now … I'll speak to you later.

[pause]

tone

[The recording is repeated.]

[pause]

That's the end of Part One.
Now turn to Part Two.

PART 2 *You will hear Ian Anderson of the Shoppers' Association talking about a problem people may face when buying some kinds of goods. For questions 9 to 18, complete the notes.*

You now have forty-five seconds in which to look at Part Two.

[pause]

tone

Ian Anderson: While most people trust that what they buy off the shelf in their local shop will be as described and brand new, there seems to be a growing trade in second-hand goods actually being sold as new. Shoppers' Association members are worried that the increasing number of used goods being discovered on offer in shops represent just the tip of the iceberg. I've dealt with over 40 cases of this kind in my area this year and, as it seems that this practice is on the increase, today's talk is aimed at keeping you all on the look out.

So, why is it happening? I think one of the main reasons is that if customers aren't satisfied with their goods, shops just give them their money back. Now, sometimes the goods are faulty, but clearly customers take advantage of this for all sorts of reasons. Often people just decide that they don't like them after a while. Then, the shopkeeper is left with what may be perfectly good used items on his hands and, of course, he wants to sell them again.

Now, some goods are much more likely to be passed off in this way than others. We've noticed that it is common with electrical goods, for example, less so with clothing, toys and so forth. For instance, we recently had a case reported to us where a washing machine was sold as new, but it was actually described in the shop as a 'Manager's Special'. No one thought to ask what that meant, and what it actually meant was that it had been used before and returned for some reason. So, when the new owner called in the repairer, because in fact it didn't work properly, he found someone else's sock inside! Now, that lady had been quite convinced that her machine was new and the shop was later fined four thousand pounds by the court.

So, what advice are we giving to people buying goods of this kind in order for them to avoid getting into this situation in the first place? Firstly, people really need to be aware of what is going on in the shop. Look at how the product is being advertised. Expressions like 'Manager's Special' or 'display model' should warn people to be, at least, suspicious. Ask what it means exactly.

After that there are other things we should be on the look out for. I think, clearly, if some of the documents are missing, which seems to be the case with a lot of these items, the guarantee's not there or there are no instructions, that sort of thing, I think it's reasonable to ask the shop what the situation is, what's happened to it. Another common situation is where the box is obviously not new or possibly damaged in some way and that should ring alarm bells too.

Expressions like 'Manager's Special' don't break the law in themselves, at least not just by saying that, unless they go on to give the impression that the goods are actually new when they are not. So, as that's often the clear impression that people go away with, what we should always do if there's any doubt, is to ask lots of questions. That will put us in the best position to know exactly what we're buying.

[pause]

tone

Now you'll hear Part Two again.

[The recording is repeated.]

[pause]

That's the end of Part Two.
Now turn to Part Three.

PART 3   *You'll hear five people talking about what they did on holiday. For questions 19 to 23, choose from the list of activities A to F which each of them is describing. Use the letters only once. There's one extra letter which you do not need to use.*

You now have thirty seconds in which to look at Part Three.

[pause]

tone

Speaker 1:   It was really through college, you see I'd studied this history course and they were organising a tour especially to visit some of the places we'd talked about. My friends thought I was mad, it didn't match their idea of energetic holidays, you know, they were off on mountain adventures and doing watersports but actually, it was quite tiring.

[pause]

Speaker 2:   I've always enjoyed being outdoors so hiring a boat for a week seemed the perfect thing to do. Bill wasn't too sure at first – he really wanted to do a bike tour of Scotland, but I promised we'd do that next year. Anyway, once he got used to wind direction and how to steer and things, he really enjoyed it.

[pause]

Speaker 3:   I wanted to do something different from lying on the beach and visiting museums. So I booked a few nights in various hotels along the route and we took the train to a starting point. It's very cheap to take your bike on the train. It was hard work at first, all that exercise, my legs really ached but apart from a couple of flat tyres we didn't have any problems.

[pause]

Speaker 4:   I went for some practice sessions first. It's very important to get the technique right – body position and using your legs to help you turn. Anyway we had a great time, no accidents, I nearly broke my leg last year when I fell off a horse! This time was fine, the snow conditions were perfect and the lifts weren't too busy. It was wonderful, I'll definitely go again.

[pause]

Speaker 5:   The mountains are such a wonderful place to go. Although they're beautiful covered in snow, I prefer them in summer – the scenery is so different. We planned our routes in the evening and set off early every morning. Of course, I made sure I had comfortable boots and that we weren't carrying too much. We kept away from the road and just used the paths, we hardly saw anyone.

[pause]

tone

Now you'll hear Part Three again.

[The recording is repeated.]

[pause]

That's the end of Part Three.
Now turn to Part Four.

PART 4   *You'll hear part of a radio programme about people who become rich quickly. Ann is telling her story. For questions 24 to 30 decide whether the statements are TRUE or FALSE. Write T for True or F for False.*

You now have one minute in which to look at Part Four.

[pause]

tone

Ann: I was brought up in a very ordinary but very happy home with one elder sister, my mother and my father. The great love of my life since I was a small girl was writing, which my family thought was surprising because they didn't consider themselves educated people. I wasn't surprised though because my parents were great readers which is my idea of being educated. Anyway, I trained to be a nurse but whenever I had free time I wrote: poems, short stories, I even once wrote a novel called 'The Pleasure Principle' but I didn't feel comfortable writing longer pieces and I soon went back to my poetry.

Then the strangest thing happened. I had my twenty-first birthday just a few days before and I was feeling very much that I wanted to change things in my life. I'd been nursing a very old woman for several months in a private ward, she told me that although she had lots of relatives, no one came to visit her. Anyway, when she died she left me an enormous sum of money, nearly three-quarters of a million pounds! Of course when the lawyer rang me up and told me I just laughed and thought that my friends were playing a joke on me. So I put down the phone and went in to tell my mother the joke.

But it wasn't a joke! All of a sudden, I was a very rich woman. Well, the first thing was that I was determined that I wouldn't waste the money. Of course I wanted to do something for my family, but all my dad said was 'We're not leaving this house after all the work I've put into the garden!' My mother agreed so all I did was give them something towards a new car and a new greenhouse. My sister was working abroad at this time and when I wrote to tell her the news and offer her some money she said it was *my* money and that she knew I would use it sensibly. None of this really came as a surprise because they've always had a sensible attitude towards money.

But this left me a fortune on my hands to spend! It soon became obvious to me that much as I loved nursing, I loved writing more and that's how I got started. I went to America and did a degree in creative writing. I had a wonderful time and learned a great deal, not from the lecturers necessarily but mainly from other hopeful writers on the course. All this was a decade ago and I've now had several volumes of poetry published. I now want to do something to help other young poets so I'm thinking of setting up a small publishing company which I'll call Grace Park Books after the wonderful old lady who helped me fulfil my life's ambition!

[pause]

tone

Now you'll hear Part Four again.

[The recording is repeated.]

[pause]

That is the end of Part Four.

There'll now be a pause of five minutes for you to copy your answers onto the separate answer sheet. I'll remind you when there is one minute left, so that you're sure to finish in time.

[pause]

You have one more minute left.

[pause]

That's the end of the test. Please stop now. Your supervisor will now collect all the question papers and answer sheets.
Goodbye.

Book 3 Test 4 Key

Paper 1 Reading (1 hour 15 minutes)

Part 1

1 F   2 H   3 D   4 E   5 G   6 B   7 A

Part 2

8 B   9 B   10 D   11 C   12 A   13 C   14 D

Part 3

15 G   16 E   17 A   18 C   19 D   20 B

Part 4

21 A   22 E   23 H   24/25 E/F *(in any order)*   26/27 B/E *(in any order)*
28 G   29 I   30 C   31 B   32 I   33 G   34/35 F/I *(in any order)*

Paper 2 Writing (1 hour 30 minutes)

Task-specific mark schemes

Question 1

Content
Reply to the friend's letter, accepting the invitation to stay, talking about own preferences and covering the points in the notes: timing; question about the climate; request for advice on clothes to bring; question about the amount of travelling planned. Should convey some enthusiasm/excitement. **NB** Candidate has not been to the country concerned before.

Organisation and cohesion
Clear paragraphing. Opening should refer to original letter and ending look forward to the visit.

Register and format
Informal letter.

Range
Phrases of thanks and enthusiastic acceptance. Language of suggestion. Variety of requests for information. Vocabulary relating to travel/holidays.

Target reader
Would be pleased to hear from the friend and be able to reply to the questions asked.

Question 2 Composition

Content
Composition should give opinions on the topic, giving a balanced argument about the money earned by sports people. **NB** Question could be interpreted as own views or views of the class as a whole.

Range
Phrases to introduce an argument. Language of opinion. Vocabulary relating to money and sport.

Organisation and cohesion
Clear presentation of ideas. Definite conclusion.

Register and format
Neutral, layout of conventional composition.

Target reader
Would be interested and informed.

Question 3 Article

Content
Article should give own and/or friends' views about the importance of clothes and whether there is a connection between what people wear and their personalities.

Range
Phrases to introduce an argument. Language of description. Vocabulary relating to clothes. Adjectives to describe personality.

Organisation and cohesion
Title desirable. Some early attempt to engage the reader, as this is an article. Clear presentation of ideas. Summary conclusion.

Register and format
Consistently informal or neutral.

Target reader
Would be interested and informed.

Question 4 Report

Content
Report should comment on the organisation of the film festival, including both the problems and the successes.

Range
Phrases to introduce positive and negative features. Narrative. Language of evaluation, description and opinion. Vocabulary to do with the cinema/festival events.

Organisation and cohesion
Clear presentation of ideas, though sub-headings not necessary. Definite conclusion.

Register and format
Formal or semi-formal, as suitable for the Club committee.

Target reader
Would be interested and informed.

Question 5 Background reading texts

(a)
Content
Description of the new character. Explanation of how the character could be added to the story and what effect this would have on the story.

Range
Language of description/summarising and explanation.
Possible use of modals.

Organisation and cohesion
Linking of description and explanation.

Appropriacy of register and format
Neutral; composition layout.

Target reader
Would know something about the character to be added, and would understand how the addition of this character would affect the story.

(b)
Content
Description of the cover. Explanation of the cover's significance to the book. An opinion on the extent to which the cover would attract a new reader to the book.

Range
Language of description, explanation and opinion.

Organisation and cohesion
Linking of description, explanation and opinion.

Appropriacy of register and format
Neutral; composition layout.

Target reader
Would have an idea of the book cover and its relevance to the book, and would know whether the writer believes the cover would attract a potential reader to the book.

Paper 3 Use of English (1 hour 15 minutes)

Part 1

1 D	2 C	3 A	4 B	5 A	6 B	7 B	8 C	9 A
10 D	11 A	12 C	13 A	14 D	15 A			

Part 2

16 in/during   17 have   18 known   19 if/whether (*allow*) how
20 spend/take   21 for   22 be   23 what   24 the
25 without   26 or   27 how   28 a   29 yourself   30 and

Part 3

Award one mark for each correct section.
31 if (1) it hadn't/had not been (1)
32 in order (1) to (1)
33 is a (1) waste of (1)
34 not be necessary (1) for you (1)
35 was funnier (1) than my friend (1)
36 cannot read (1) the newspaper without (1)
37 behave (1) so badly that OR (1) are so badly behaved (1) that (1)
38 was (very) lucky (1) not to (1)
39 anyone (else) anybody/a single person (1) apart from (1)
40 thought (that) Peter (1) was unlikely (1)

Part 4

41 ✓   42 ✓   43 other   44 never   45 years   46 most
47 ✓   48 on   49 ✓   50 too   51 ✓   52 eat   53 time
54 been   55 that

Part 5

56 paintings   57 artist   58 impressive   59 connections
60 surrounding   61 opening   62 unfortunately   63 illness
64 daily   65 admission/admittance

Paper 4 Listening (40 minutes approximately)

Part 1
1 C   2 A   3 C   4 B   5 C   6 B   7 A   8 A

Part 2
9 house   10 the first floor/up a ladder   11 old roses
12 (wonderful) scent(s)/smell(s)   13 mother(-)in(-)law
14 the Children of Riverside   15 drew (the) pictures
16 (the) rooms   17 peace (and quiet)
18 (200) (beautiful) (old) cushion(s)

Part 3
19 E   20 C   21 A   22 F   23 D

Part 4
24 A   25 M   26 S   27 S   28 S   29 M   30 A

Transcript *First Certificate Listening Test. Test Four.*
Hello. I'm going to give you the instructions for this test. I'll introduce each part of the test and give you time to look at the questions. At the start of each piece you'll hear this sound.

tone

You'll hear each piece twice.

Remember, while you're listening, write your answers on the question paper. You'll have time at the end of the test to copy your answers onto the separate answer sheet.

The tape will now be stopped. Please ask any questions now, because you must not speak during the test.

[pause]

PART 1 *Now open your question paper and look at Part One.*
You'll hear people talking in eight different situations. For questions 1 to 8, choose the best answer, A, B or C.

Question 1 One
Listen to this man talking to his friend about a meeting. Who turned up at the meeting?
A *Marian*
B *James*
C *Alison*

[pause]

tone

Pete: Hi Marian. What happened to you last night? I thought you were coming to the meeting.
Marian: Was it last night, Pete? Oh, I'm sorry. I completely forgot about it. How did it go?
Pete: Well, it was a bit embarrassing really. There were only two of us. Alison was supposed to be bringing James but he wasn't feeling very well. So she came on her own.
Marian: A bit of a waste of time then?
Pete: Yes – we'd better arrange another meeting on …

[pause]

tone

[The recording is repeated.]

[pause]

Question 2 Two
You hear a man complaining about the place where he works. What is the problem in the office?
A *the heat*
B *the noise*
C *the pollution*

[pause]

tone

Man:　We have air-conditioning in our office, but because it's not regulated round the floors, on some floors it might be on and on other floors it mightn't be on. It can be quite off-putting. I work on a computer all day, so I've got a fan going all the time which blows all the papers round the room, and the window's open, although we're not supposed to. Because really, in our office, you know, it's quite airless even when it's on.

[pause]

tone

[The recording is repeated.]

[pause]

Question 3　*Three*
You hear somebody talking about choosing a name for something. What is he talking about?
A　a children's toy
B　a computer game
C　a rock band

[pause]

tone

Man:　I think the first time I ever really thought about names was when I had to pick one for a group that I'd put together and we picked a terrible name, we called ourselves Buggles. In our heads we saw ourselves as a sort of product from a huge futuristic factory that manufactured compact discs and the Buggles were kind of little robots. It all sounds a bit childish now, doesn't it? If we'd called ourselves something better, well, we might well have sold millions, but when you're called the Buggles, nobody's interested in you.

[pause]

tone

[The recording is repeated.]

[pause]

Question 4　*Four*
You hear somebody talking about the sport of badminton. What point is she making about the sport?
A　It's very popular.
B　It can be dangerous.
C　It's quite exciting.

[pause]

tone

Woman:　Forget about skiing and mountain climbing. If you're looking for a sport to inject a little risk into your life, try badminton. For every thousand people who enjoy playing the game in their spare time, thirty-six find themselves laid up with a serious injury according to a recent survey. Nearly half of those were sprains and strains, but knocks and falls were also factors.

[pause]

tone

[The recording is repeated.]

[pause]

Question 5 *Five*
A friend tells you about the time he was robbed. What was his feeling about the incident?
A He felt surprised.
B He felt angry.
C He felt lucky.

[pause]

tone

Man: People tell me that that's an incredibly safe area but you know I'm never surprised when things go missing from hotel rooms. I mean I would've been really angry if they'd taken my passport and everything but when it's only traveller's cheques I don't think I did too badly.

[pause]

tone

[The recording is repeated.]

[pause]

Question 6 *Six*
You hear the beginning of a radio programme. What is the programme going to be about?
A farming
B baking
C building

[pause]

tone

Radio presenter: It's a very English scene. A soft summer rain and open countryside as far as the eye can see. I'm in the small village of Batby, on the village green, with a farmer's tractor just behind me, and in front of me the village bakery, a squat, two-storey building built out of local stone, and next to it a pale white house with large windows. And the reason I'm here is because I think that this village probably produces the best bread in the whole of the country, and to prove it there are cars parked all around the little shop that is run by Andy, who I've come to see.

[pause]

tone

[The recording is repeated.]

[pause]

Question 7   *Seven*
Listen to this man talking on the radio. Who is he?
A an ambulance driver
B a weatherman
C a policeman

[pause]

tone

Man: Good evening. I'm very glad to be able to speak to you all this evening. In fact, on the way to the studio, the weather was so bad I didn't think I was going to make it. But this is one thing I want to talk about this evening – getting from one place to another despite the weather. Accidents are often caused by atrocious conditions – snow, ice, freezing fog – and what makes our job difficult is getting to the injured people as quickly as possible so that we can begin treating them. This means that we need training in …

[pause]

tone

[The recording is repeated.]

[pause]

Question 8   *Eight*
Listen to this teacher talking about hiring bicycles. Why is he speaking?
A to give a warning
B to change some plans
C to provide some directions

[pause]

tone

Man: Before you all dash off to hire bicycles for this weekend, you might like to think again! The town is very busy at this time of the year and there's a lot of traffic on the roads. There are a lot of visitors who aren't sure where they're going and are often likely to suddenly change their mind. So, if you do go out, make sure you pay attention at all times.

[pause]

tone

[The recording is repeated.]

[pause]

That's the end of Part One.
Now turn to Part Two.

PART 2   *You'll hear an interview with a woman called Diana Walton at the old house which is her family home. For questions 9 to 18, complete each of the sentences.*

You now have forty-five seconds in which to look at Part Two.

[pause]

tone

Interviewer: It's a glorious summer's day and I'm looking out over a typical English country garden. I'm at Riverside House and I'm sitting with its owner, Diana Walton. Diana, it's got quite a claim to fame this house, hasn't it?

Diana: It has indeed. It is the oldest house in Britain that was built as a house, there are some older ones that started off as castles, but this one has always been just a house. It was built in 1130 and much of the original house still remains.

Interviewer: And which room is this that we're sitting in?

Diana: Yes, we're now sitting in the hall on the first floor and this was, in fact, the room through which you would have entered the house in 1130, because the front door was then on the first floor, up a ladder which they pulled in after them for safety. And here we are surrounded by the original stone walls, still with the arches.

Interviewer: And surrounded by this beautiful garden.

Diana: Yes, it has one of the best collections of old roses in the country, and goes right down to the river. It was laid out by Emily Watson, it was a green field when she came here, but she loved scented plants and certainly everyone who comes here comments on the wonderful smells in the garden.

Interviewer: You mentioned Emily Watson who is, of course, more famous for her children's books.

Diana: Yes, she was my mother-in-law in fact, and she first came here when she was fifteen, although it was only at the age of sixty-two that she wrote her first book called, 'The Children of Riverside'. It was based on the house and she wove into the stories descriptions of the house, the gardens and many things in the house itself.

Interviewer: Which you can still see?

Diana: Oh yes. Her son Peter actually drew pictures in the book and they're quite faithful to what was described, which is, after all, what is still here.

Interviewer: And do you get visits from fans of the books?

Diana: Certainly. It's absolutely magical for readers of the books to be able to come and walk into the world they've read about. There's always a gasp of pleasure when people walk in and recognise the rooms described in the books.

Interviewer: Do you get many visitors?

Diana: Yes, we're open to the public on summer Saturdays and people come to see the house and gardens. The house always gives people enormous pleasure whether or not they know the books because it has such a feeling of peace and quiet.

Interviewer: Mmm, it certainly does. And also on the sofa here are some of the many beautiful old cushions that seem to be everywhere.

Diana: That's right. Emily Watson made a collection of over two hundred old cushions, many of them made in this house over the centuries and they're becoming very well known internationally and some visitors come because they know there's such an important collection here.

Interviewer: Diana, thank you so much for letting us visit your house today.

Diana: It's been my pleasure.

[pause]

tone

Now you'll hear Part Two again.

[The recording is repeated.]

[pause]

That's the end of Part Two.
Now turn to Part Three.

PART 3 *You'll hear five different men talking about silence. For questions 19 to 23, choose from the list A to F who is speaking. Use the letters only once. There is one extra letter which you do not need to use.*

You now have thirty seconds in which to look at Part Three.

[pause]

tone

Speaker 1: Silences can be worrying because the fear arises in your listeners that something has gone wrong. What every broadcaster is taught to avoid is dead air. Dead air is something which bores, whereas a meaningful silence is important. Without a certain amount of silence, broadcasting would be terribly unrelaxing. But the big fear is, you know, especially on the late night show, you put on a song and you pop out to go to the bathroom or for a sandwich and you don't quite get back in time.

[pause]

Speaker 2: To get to the heart of a piece you have to discover its breathing-in moments, the listening moments. When you're on stage and not speaking, you have to teach yourself to stay in the role, and you have to look natural; and to do that you have to think of all the reasons why you are not speaking at that moment. Then when your line comes, you have to feel very desperate to speak at that moment. If not, why were you silent for so long?

[pause]

Speaker 3: We definitely set out to make witnesses nervous by remaining silent in the hope that the person will go on to say something which is particularly useful to us. There is a type of silence which is important and which is normally controlled by the professionals in court because they know what they're doing, and they've been taught to keep silent, so that the other person will carry on speaking, will fill the gap. So, if you ever have to go to court, it's essential to learn that when you've finished speaking, you shut up!

[pause]

Speaker 4: All my training makes me want to get someone talking and keep them talking, to fill the space, to make them finish. But actually silence is essential to a human voice telling you something interesting. It may mean your guest is hiding something, or sometimes waiting to decide whether to say something in front of the camera. So, there's the silence that you leave because something interesting may be coming, and there's the silence that you wait for because people sometimes repeat things to give them emphasis, or change things slightly.

[pause]

Speaker 5: For me, it's a question of concentration. When I'm on court, I need to think very carefully about what I'm doing. People think it's all physical strength and speed, but to play well you actually have to think it through, plan your next shot, get your opponent on the wrong foot. So when someone in the crowd laughs or coughs and breaks my concentration, I get really mad. But you can't show that, it's a lesson in self control, in learning not to be put off by things.

[pause]

tone

Now you'll hear Part Three again.

[The recording is repeated.]

[pause]

That's the end of Part Three.
Now turn to Part Four.

PART 4 *You'll hear a conversation between three people who are organising a sports day in their village. For questions 24 to 30, write S for Susan, A for Alan or M for Marie.*

You now have forty-five seconds in which to look at Part Four.

[pause]

tone

Susan: Right, let's get started shall we? Thanks for coming Alan and Marie, I know how busy you both are. Now, we decided at the last meeting that the basic programme would be a sports day with a disco later in the evening.

Alan: I've been thinking Susan, we need to get someone interesting to open the event, don't we? You know, make a speech.

Susan: Yes, I was just coming to that, any ideas?

Alan: Well, there's a chap at my running club who's just been in an International competition. We could ask him.

Marie: That sounds good. I couldn't come up with anyone.

Susan: Decided then, make a note of that Alan. Now the next item is the children's games. We need someone to be in charge of them in the day. Marie?

Marie: I'll do that if you like. I'm sure I'll enjoy running the competitions.

Susan: It'll be hard work – I know, I've done it before. Now, if I were you Marie, I'd make sure I had plenty of helpers and don't let that Mick Brown get involved or he'll take over.

Marie: I'll remember that Susan. What about the hall, for the evening do?

Alan: We have a problem there. Mr Taylor says it's not available that evening, something to do with it being repainted, he's worried about the paint getting marked.

Susan: Nonsense, he's just making excuses. Go and see him again and insist we need it that evening.

Alan: OK. By the way Susan, did you find out about that disco you mentioned?

Susan: Oh no, I completely forgot. Sorry, look I'll definitely do that tomorrow and let you both know immediately.

Marie:	We need to make a decision about the food too.
Susan:	Yes, that's next on my agenda. Now I think we should have a hot meal. That would be nice, there are plenty of tables and chairs for everyone.
Marie:	I don't think that's practical. You'd just make more work for everyone. A few sandwiches is much easier.
Susan:	I suppose you're right. Put that down Alan. Did anyone remember to ask about getting the invitations printed?
Marie:	I couldn't get through on the phone.
Susan:	Alan?
Alan:	I got a rough estimate for the cost. The printer says if we let him have the exact details, he'll give us a price.
Susan:	Well done, that's about it for tonight. If we meet again on Friday, we can finalise all the details.

[pause]

tone

Now you'll hear Part Four again.

[The recording is repeated.]

[pause]

That is the end of Part Four.

There'll now be a pause of five minutes for you to copy your answers onto the separate answer sheet. I'll remind you when there's one minute left, so that you're sure to finish in time.

[pause]

You have one more minute left.

[pause]

That's the end of the test. Please stop now. Your supervisor will now collect all the question papers and answer sheets.
Goodbye.

Book 4 Test 1 Key

Paper 1 Reading (1 hour 15 minutes)

Part 1
1 D   2 B   3 F   4 H   5 G   6 E   7 A

Part 2
8 C   9 A   10 B   11 D   12 C   13 A   14 C

Part 3
15 D   16 B   17 C   18 A   19 E   20 H   21 G

Part 4
22/23 C/D (*in any order*)   24 F   25 A   26 B   27 E   28 C
29 E   30 F   31 B   32 E   33/34 C/D (*in any order*)   35 C

Paper 2 Writing (1 hour 30 minutes)

Task-specific mark schemes

Question 1
Content
Major points: Letter should clearly state the reason for writing i.e. the writer
wants the friend to join the group on holiday. Must cover essential information
about the house, price and dates. Letter must mention at least one place of local
interest and one thing to do.
Minor points: Any additional information.

Organisation and cohesion
Clear opening to letter. Suitable paragraphing. Appropriate ending.

Appropriacy of register and format
Informal letter.

Range
Language of description. Future tenses. Vocabulary relating to holidays. Some
expression of persuasion.

Target reader
Would have a clear idea of the house and holiday and would consider joining
the group of friends.

Question 2

Content
Clear indication of the person and why important (**NB** Could be a relative as long as importance to **country** is explained). Explanation of what kind of influence the person has had.

Range
Language of description and explanation. Tenses should be appropriate i.e. according to whether the person is still alive or deceased.

Organisation and cohesion
Clear linking between the person and the influence, the description and the explanation.

Appropriacy of register and format
Article format i.e. some paragraphing. Neutral/formal register.

Target reader
Would have a clear picture of the person chosen and their influence on the country.

Question 3

Content
Agree, disagree or both. Should be some mention of the writer's experiences.

Range
Language of opinion, explanation, justification. Vocabulary related to education.

Organisation and cohesion
Clear linking between opinions and writer's experience. Some logical development of ideas.

Appropriacy of register and format
Neutral. Composition format. Some paragraphing essential.

Target reader
Would understand the writer's point of view.

Question 4

Content
Report should identify by name/location/type and then describe at least two places to eat and drink in the town. Explanation of their suitability to students from other countries.

Range
Language of description and explanation. Vocabulary relating to food/drink or setting/ambiance or both.

Organisation and cohesion
Information could be presented in two or more paragraphs/sections. The report must establish the link between place and suitability.

Appropriacy of register and format
Register consistent throughout. Could be informal (student connection).
Sub-headings an advantage, but not essential.

Target reader
Would know of at least two suitable places where the students could eat and
drink.

Question 5(a)

Content
Clear reference to three surprising things in the book and why these were
chosen.

Range
Language of description and explanation.

Organisation and cohesion
Linking of description and explanation.

Appropriacy of register and format
Neutral. Composition layout.

Target reader
Would know why the writer has chosen these three things. (**NB** A thing could
be a person in this context.)

Question 5(b)

Content
Clear reference to the role to be played and why.

Range
Language of description and explanation.

Organisation and cohesion
Linking of description and explanation.

Appropriacy of register and format
Neutral. Composition layout.

Target reader
Would understand why the writer would want to play the chosen role in a film.

Paper 3   Use of English (1 hour 15 minutes)

Part 1
1 A   2 D   3 A   4 B   5 D   6 B   7 B   8 C   9 C
10 D   11 A   12 C   13 D   14 C   15 A

Part 2
16 of   17 which   18 been   19 them/all/these   20 who
21 with   22 where   23 for   24 this/that   25 from   26 or
27 is   28 its   29 so   30 are

Part 3

Award one mark for each correct section.

31 isn't/is not (1) interested in (1)
32 must not (1) be fed (1)
33 was John's first (1) visit to (1)
34 told Anne (1) (that) he would (1)
35 not (1) as many students (1)
36 mistook/took me (1) for (1) OR confused me (1) with (1) OR believed/
    supposed me (1) to be (1)
37 would/'d (1) like to (1)
38 (his) being unable (1) to swim (1)
39 is no/not a (1) chance of (1)
40 if you (1) had not written (1) OR without you(r) (1) writing/having
    written (1)

Part 4

41 had   42 ✓   43 being   44 much   45 ✓   46 the   47 ✓
48 ✓   49 my   50 ✓   51 about   52 all   53 time   54 while
55 ourselves

Part 5

56 observation(s)   57 behaviour   58 association   59 saying
60 surprisingly   61 unlikely   62 useful 63 P/proof   64 sunshine
65 daily

Paper 4   Listening (40 minutes approximately)

Part 1

1 A   2 B   3 C   4 A   5 C   6 B   7 A   8 A

Part 2

9 (fairly/very) late   10 discovery/discovering centre   11 feel box
12 careful   13 activity day(s)   14 our planet
15 environment(al) (issues)   16 (a guided) tour   17 (a) tea party
18 (a bag of) gift(s)

Part 3

19 F   20 D   21 A   22 C   23 E

Part 4

24 T   25 T   26 T   27 F   28 F   29 F   30 F

Transcript   *First Certificate Listening Test. Test One.*
Hello. I'm going to give you the instructions for this test. I'll introduce each part of the test and give you time to look at the questions. At the start of each piece you'll hear this sound.

tone

You'll hear each piece twice.

Remember, while you're listening, write your answers on the question paper. You'll have time at the end of the test to copy your answers onto the separate answer sheet.

The tape will now be stopped. Please ask any questions now, because you must not speak during the test.

[pause]

PART 1   *Now open your question paper and look at Part One.*

[pause]

You'll hear people talking in eight different situations. For questions 1 to 8, choose the best answer, A, B or C.

Question 1   *One*
You hear a young man talking to his friend about a film. What is his opinion of the film?
A It was too long.
B The acting was poor.
C There was too much violence.

[pause]

tone

Man: ... mm ... well, no, I can't say I really enjoyed it at all that much. I don't go to the cinema much, but I did make the effort for this, because I'd quite enjoyed the book even though I thought it was a bit violent.
Friend: Oh, is it?
Man: Mm, though they'd cut out a lot of that in the film.
Friend: Ah.
Man: Yes ... It had some good people in it and they did their best – you couldn't blame the actors – but honestly it went on and on, by the time it finally ended, I was just longing to get out and have a cup of coffee to wake me up!

[pause]

tone

[The recording is repeated.]

[pause]

Question 2   *Two*
You hear part of an interview with a man on the radio. What is the man talking about?
A shopping
B gardening
C painting

[pause]

tone

Interviewer: ... and how about the apples?

Man: Oh, yes – wonderful, and quite easy, too. Some varieties are better than others, of course. It depends what size, colour and texture you're looking for in the apples themselves and obviously the size and shape of the tree are important, too, according to where you want to put it. It's a question of proportion. But nothing beats your own apples – you'll never get them from the supermarket again!

[pause]

tone

[The recording is repeated.]

[pause]

Question 3   *Three*
You hear a man talking about his job. Where does he work?
A in a hotel
B in a travel agent's
C in a shop

[pause]

tone

Man: Well, we get a lot of tourists from Europe, and Japan, and then we also get a lot of people from cities outside of New York. And then we also get a lot of New Yorkers and people who are very fashion-conscious and very well-to-do. And then we also get customers who are people who normally don't dress this way but they find a certain piece that really excites them. Like if they see a certain shirt or a certain skirt and then just say 'Oh, this is wonderful' and they'll have to get it.

[pause]

tone

[The recording is repeated.]

[pause]

Question 4   *Four*
You hear Jessica telling a friend about a trip. Why is she going to Japan?
A to do some painting
B to learn Japanese
C to study Japanese art

[pause]

tone

Male:	Japan! Sounds exciting. Business or pleasure, Jessica?
Jessica:	Well, *some* pleasure, but the trip's being paid for, so it's really business.
Male:	Did you win a scholarship or something?
Jessica:	No, although I expect or, rather, I hope I'll learn some Japanese while I'm there, but in fact this language school in Tokyo wants me to do a big picture in each of eight rooms to show English life and scenery.

[pause]

tone

[The recording is repeated.]

[pause]

Question 5   *Five*
In a hospital waiting room, you hear this conversation. What is the man doing?
A making a complaint
B expressing approval
C making a suggestion

[pause]

tone

Male:	Excuse me. Have you got a minute? Um ... I've been waiting for ages and I was wondering ...
Female:	The doctors *are* very busy ...
Male:	No, no, no, it's not that. It's just that I'm rather thirsty after all this time. Have you thought of getting a drinks machine put in?
Female:	Uhm. I'll speak to the hospital management about that. I don't think so actually.

[pause]

tone

[The recording is repeated.]

[pause]

Question 6   *Six*
              You hear some friends talking. How does the woman feel?
              A worried
              B annoyed
              C disappointed

              [pause]

              tone

Woman:	Look, it's already eight o'clock and Tom said he'd be here by seven.
Man:	Yes, but you know what the traffic is like at this time of the evening.
Woman:	He said he'd make a special effort not to be late. Why does he always do this?
Man:	Keep your hair on. There's probably a reasonable explanation.
Woman:	You mean he'll give us one of his typical excuses. Well, I've had enough this time.

              [pause]

              tone

              [The recording is repeated.]

              [pause]

Question 7   *Seven*
              You overhear two people talking in a café. What is the relationship between
              them?
              A They belong to the same club.
              B They are students together.
              C They work for the same company.

              [pause]

              tone

Man 1:	It's good to get out and do something active at lunchtimes, isn't it?
Man 2:	Yeah, I look forward to our games. And the courts and stuff are pretty good, aren't they, considering how little it costs to join.
Man 1:	Yeah, I'm glad we decided to, of course. I'm still learning but I'll beat you one day!
Man 2:	Oh yeah? Anyway, I'd better get back, I've got to give a talk this afternoon.
Man 1:	Yeah, I've been meaning to ask you, what's it like at your place these days?
Man 2:	Much like yours I should think, dead boring. It's not what I thought I'd end up doing when I was at college.

              [pause]

              tone

              [The recording is repeated.]

              [pause]

Question 8   *Eight*
You hear part of a radio programme on the subject of films. What is special about the music in John Hunt's film?
A *It holds your attention.*
B *It follows the action.*
C *It stays in your memory.*

[pause]

tone

Man: Film music is like another voice which is telling you part of the story. Certain types are given names, like 'Mickey Mousing', for example, where the music directly follows the action on the screen. The films of John Hunt, however, are known for their minimalist music, which is three or four notes in repetition, a great deal of repetition, and, after a while, this begins to work on the emotions of the audience and as you're sitting in the cinema you get tense and more involved in what's going on on the screen.

[pause]

tone

[The recording is repeated.]

[pause]

That is the end of Part One.

Now turn to Part Two.

PART 2   *You'll hear part of a nature programme for young people in Britain. For questions 9 to 18, fill in the missing information.*

You now have forty-five seconds in which to look at Part Two.

[pause]

tone

Kathy: OK, now it's time for our regular slot 'Nature Notes', and as usual Paul Sinclair is here to tell us about some of the things you can look out for at the moment. Paul, I believe the Natural History Museum in London has something of particular interest at the moment.
Paul: Yes, they have. They've got what they call 'Dinosaur Safari', which is an exhibition that takes you back to the time when those pre-historic creatures were around. With the use of high technology, they've created some realistic moving dinosaurs that can be pretty scary, I warn you! One tip I would give you, though, is to get to the exhibition fairly late to miss the worst of the queues. After all, there's plenty more to see in the museum before that.
Kathy: What about for people who can't get to London for that?
Paul: Yes, for those of you out of easy reach of London, the museum also has something called the Discovery Centre, which visits venues around the country and is particularly aimed at young people. One great thing is that they have specimens you can touch such as bones and stuffed animals. And one thing that's proved particularly popular is known as the 'feel box' where you identify mystery objects by touch only. So try to get along to the centre when it comes to your area.

Kathy:	Now, there's something for budding geologists, isn't there?
Paul:	Yes, it's a project called 'Rockwatch' and the idea is to encourage young people to be *careful* collectors of rocks. The organisers say that *careless* collecting can easily damage sites and that the youngsters could teach the grown-ups a thing or two about that. Anyone aged between 8 and 18 can join Rockwatch, which will give them a chance to learn about fossils, dinosaurs and so on. And also they'll be able to go along to activity days, where they can take part in all sorts of exciting things.
Kathy:	You've got something about a writing competition next, haven't you?
Paul:	Yes, that's right, it's called 'Our Planet'. It's being run by the Society for the Protection of Birds and it's open to anyone up to the age of 20. They've called it 'Our Planet' because it doesn't just concern birds. It can be anything to do with the environment. If you want to enter, you have to write a 400-word article on an environmental issue that's close to your heart and send it to them before July 30. The prize is certainly well worth having – a word processor that will be great for anyone who's keen to be a writer.
Kathy:	OK, and finally, exciting things are happening at Edinburgh Zoo, aren't they?
Paul:	They certainly are. On June 18, they're holding an open day for young people. You'll get a guided tour in the morning and there'll be quizzes and demonstrations during the afternoon. After that there's a tea party at one of the city's biggest hotels, which should be great fun. Tickets cost £10 and for that you also get a bag of gifts, so it's well worth the money.
Kathy:	OK, thanks Paul. You can get details of everything that . . .

[pause]

tone

Now you'll hear Part Two again.

[The recording is repeated.]

[pause]

That's the end of Part Two.

Now turn to Part Three.

PART 3   *You will hear five people talking about experiences connected with school. For questions 19 to 23, choose from the list A to F what each speaker says about his or her school days. Use the letters only once. There is one extra letter which you do not need to use.*

You now have thirty seconds in which to look at Part Three.

[pause]

tone

Speaker 1:	It may have a great reputation, especially for football, but I only went there because my parents insisted I had to go. I met a lot of people who've been useful to me in later life, but apart from that it was a waste of time for me. I suppose I enjoyed the woodwork, but if they thought I was going to make an effort, they were wrong.

Speaker 2:   We moved from another part of the country, and I arrived in the middle of term. Everyone already had their friends, and I felt left out of everything. But Mike Trenchard really helped. He taught modern languages – which I was good at – and he really helped me fit in, despite my failures on the tennis court. I remember . . .

Speaker 3:   I wasn't really any good at things like history and maths. The one thing I did enjoy was swimming so I got chosen for the team in my first term – and then I had the confidence to try other things like fencing and athletics, and I ended up being a bit of a star.

Speaker 4:   My parents were both teachers and I was very interested in books but the school seemed more interested in training girls in cookery and needlework, where I was just hopeless. I wanted to study Latin and Greek but everyone – teachers especially – thought I was odd. I couldn't wait to leave.

Speaker 5:   It was in the fifth year, the year when we had to study really hard, and there was this boy whose brother was going out with my sister and he started spreading rumours, saying things about my parents and me. And my work was suffering and in the end the school authorities had to sort it out.

[pause]

tone

Now you'll hear Part Three again.

[The recording is repeated.]

[pause]

That's the end of Part Three.

Now turn to Part Four.

PART 4   *You will hear part of a radio interview with a famous Australian novelist, Dorothy Shields. For questions 24 to 30, decide which of the statements are TRUE and which are FALSE. Write T for True or F for False in the boxes provided.*

You now have forty-five seconds in which to look at Part Four.

[pause]

tone

Interviewer: You've just finished writing your life story, haven't you?

Dorothy: Well, Volume One actually, and I don't see how there can ever be a Volume Two because of the number of people I've known who are still alive. Now, the book I've just finished, is about people most of whom are dead or don't care.

Interviewer: So, you don't believe in giving away other people's secrets?

Dorothy: No, I absolutely do not.

Interviewer: I suppose the other reason for writing your life story is that if you don't, other people will do it for you, and, as long as you're around and able to write it yourself, it must be very annoying if they want to.

Dorothy: Well, there is a young woman writing one now. I tried to stop her, but I've given up. I thought, 'OK, if you can't beat them, join them' so that's why I wrote my book, yes.

Interviewer: But also annoying if you're capable of doing it yourself is that, however well researched it is, it's bound to be inaccurate, to a certain extent, isn't it?

Dorothy:	I also think they make things up quite a lot. Sometimes I think 'Oh, it doesn't matter', but, you know, at other times I get quite cross. But I don't know if this book is to improve things or not, because I don't know what people are expecting really.
Interviewer:	But you also tore up your first two novels, didn't you?
Dorothy:	I've torn up a lot more than that. Yes, I ripped them up and a lot of short stories too.
Interviewer:	You've gone on tearing them up?
Dorothy:	I tore one up last year actually. You know it's much better to start again than to try and change something, you see. Because you get on to a sort of, um . . . well, I don't know, a wavelength when it's going well.
Interviewer:	But if you decide that you really should begin again, why don't you just put it away somewhere, you never know, if you've spent that long working on it, isn't it a terrible thing just to throw it away?
Dorothy:	Well, if I do have a moment of doubt afterwards, I think of all the theses that might be written about it and then I'm pleased that it's not going to be studied!
Interviewer:	But, when you first came to this country, as an adult, with the manuscript of what was to be your first published novel in your suitcase, it was published and met with immediate success. Were you surprised?
Dorothy:	Well, you know, I was a very raw young woman out of the bush then. I've now become elderly and respectable, but then I was so green and when publishers phoned me up to say it had been accepted, I thought 'This must be what happens to everybody'. They saw me as extremely cool, but really I just didn't know.
Interviewer:	But, you believed you would be published?
Dorothy:	Yes, I find it very difficult now to understand my state of mind at that time. My confidence was amazing. I just knew I was going to be a writer and I was going to be published. There's a phrase that's disappeared, a 1950s phrase,'to be in for the long haul'. I was always in for the long haul, I wasn't going to give up and turn my hand to anything else, because, well as I say, what could I do?

[pause]

tone

Now you'll hear Part Four again.

[The recording is repeated.]

[pause]

That's the end of Part Four.

There'll now be a pause of five minutes for you to copy your answers onto the separate answer sheet.
I'll remind you when there is one minute left, so that you're sure to finish in time.

[pause]

You have one more minute left.

[pause]

That's the end of the test. Please stop now. Your supervisor will now collect all the question papers and answer sheets.
Goodbye.

Book 4 Test 2 Key

Paper 1   Reading (1 hour 15 minutes)

Part 1
1 C   2 F   3 E   4 A   5 H   6 B   7 G

Part 2
8 D   9 D   10 B   11 A   12 D   13 B   14 C   15 B

Part 3
16 F   17 H   18 G   19 B   20 C   21 E   22 A

Part 4
23 A   24 C   25 B   26 A   27 B   28 D   29 A   30 B
31 B   32 D   33 C   34 A   35 C

Paper 2   Writing (1 hour 30 minutes)

Task-specific mark schemes

Question 1
Content
Major points: Early explanation of who is writing and why i.e. requesting permission to hold a party. Must give precise information – date, time, place. Some reference needed to noise and tidying up.
Minor points: Who is responsible for what (Noriko, Amanda).

Organisation and cohesion
Clear opening to letter. Suitable paragraphing. Appropriate ending.

Appropriacy of register and format
Formal letter.

Range
Language of requests. Language of description and future plans. Some expression of persuasion/reassurance. Vocabulary relating to the organisation of parties.

Target reader
Would have enough information to consider the request.

Question 2

Content
Letter should include brief reference to fact that the cousin was not able to come to the wedding. Coverage of the whole day's events. Some details of the guests.

Range
Language of description for events and people. Past tenses. Vocabulary relating to wedding celebrations.

Organisation and cohesion
Clear opening to letter. Suitable paragraphing. Appropriate ending.

Appropriacy of register and format
Informal letter.

Target reader
Would have a picture of the wedding and be informed about who was there.

Question 3

Content
Story related in some way to the first day, beginning with the words given.

Range
Narrative. Past tenses. Language of description.

Organisation and cohesion
Opening sentences set the scene. Possibly only minimal paragraphing thereafter. Obvious ending.

Appropriacy of register and format
Consistently neutral or informal.

Target reader
Would be able to follow the storyline.

Question 4

Content
Suggestions of ways to remember new vocabulary in English. More than one suggestion must be given.

Range
Language of opinion and suggestion. Use of appropriate modals. Vocabulary relating to language learning.

Organisation and cohesion
Clear opening to article. Suitable paragraphing. Conclusion.

Appropriacy of register and format
More or less formal (written for college magazine) but must be consistent.

Target reader
Would be informed.

Question 5(a)

Content
Clear reference to the book. Description of two pictures and an explanation as to why they would make a suitable cover.

Range
Language of description and explanation.

Organisation and cohesion
Linking of description and explanation.

Appropriacy of register and format
Neutral. Composition layout.

Target reader
Would know why the writer thinks these two pictures would make a suitable cover.

Question 5(b)

Content
Clear reference to the book chosen. Description of the character chosen and the change(s) undergone.

Range
Language of description, opinion and explanation.

Organisation and cohesion
Linking of description, opinion and explanation.

Appropriacy of register and format
Neutral. Composition layout.

Target reader
Would understand why the writer has chosen this character.

Paper 3   Use of English (1 hour 15 minutes)

Part 1
1 A   2 D   3 B   4 B   5 C   6 D   7 C   8 B   9 D
10 A   11 C   12 A   13 C   14 D   15 B

Part 2
16 which/that   17 used   18 could/can   19 to   20 become
21 until/till/before   22 first   23 had/made/created   24 how
25 where   26 because/as/since   27 on   28 their   29 for   30 the

Part 3
Award one mark for each correct section.
31 enjoyed the film (1) apart from (1)
32 is going to (1) be pulled (1)

33 has been learning Russian (1) for (1)
34 told/instructed/commanded/ordered Rebecca (1) not to (1) OR said (that)
   Rebecca (1) must/should not (1)
35 was not/wasn't (1) as/so expensive/dear/costly as (1)
36 there was (1) no point (in) (1)
37 must (1) have/'ve been (1)
38 did not/didn't deserve (1) to be (1)
39 nothing left (1) in this/the (1)
40 was forty/40 (1) when he learned/learnt/started/began (1)

Part 4

41 as   42 ✓   43 it   44 ✓   45 go   46 so   47 the
48 they   49 to   50 ✓   51 of   52 that   53 much   54 kind
55 who

Part 5

56 carefully   57 organisations   58 majority   59 cultural
60 knowledge   61 teenagers   62 correspondence   63 obligation
64 entertainment   65 broaden

Paper 4   Listening (40 minutes approximately)

Part 1
1 B   2 B   3 B   4 A   5 C   6 A   7 C   8 C

Part 2
9 (a) painter/(an) artist   10 (the) (old) bus station
11 (a) golf champion/(champion) golfer   12 (a) furniture shop
13 engineering   14 (the) Market Hall
15 Nothing Ever Changes   16 (a) bank robbery   17 (the) Leisure Centre
18 (the) Evening Post/(the/our) local evening (news)paper

Part 3
19 F   20 D   21 A   22 E   23 B

Part 4
24 T   25 T   26 F   27 F   28 T   29 T   30 F

Transcript   *First Certificate Listening Test. Test Two.*
Hello. I'm going to give you the instructions for this test. I'll introduce each part of the test and give you time to look at the questions. At the start of each piece you'll hear this sound.

tone

You will hear each piece twice.

Remember, while you're listening, write your answers on the question paper. You'll have time at the end of the test to copy your answers onto the separate answer sheet.

The tape will now be stopped. Please ask any questions now, because you must not speak during the test.

[pause]

PART 1   *Now open your question paper and look at Part One.*

[pause]

You will hear people talking in eight different situations. For questions 1 to 8, choose the best answer, A, B or C.

Question 1   One
You hear two people discussing a play. Who is going to see it?
A the man
B both of them
C neither of them

[pause]

tone

Man: . . . well, I'm not sure. It sounds as if it might be rather violent for us.
Woman: Yes, but it's ever so famous. The director won some kind of award. Peter saw it a few months ago and according to him some of it *was* violent, but it was all done in a very matter-of-fact way – nothing too . . . um . . . you know . . .
Man: OK, then. I suppose it'll make a change from comedies.

[pause]

tone

[The recording is repeated.]

[pause]

Question 2   Two
You will hear an announcement about a television programme. What is the programme about?
A Indian religion
B Indian cooking
C Indian history

[pause]

tone

Announcer: . . . and at 8.30 there's another chance to see the last in our series 'Indian Magic'. In tonight's programme, Usha Verma travels to central India and tries some of the dishes prepared by this historic region's top cooks. She will also be giving you once again a step-by-step guide to producing similar delights at home and looking at some of the traditional dishes associated with a festival at a famous local temple.

[pause]

tone

[The recording is repeated.]

[pause]

Question 3   *Three*
Listen to this man speaking. Who is he?
A a traffic policeman
B a taxi driver
C a tour guide

[pause]

tone

Man: Well I can, but the traffic may be bad when we get nearer the centre. You'll have to walk the last hundred metres or so anyway, because I'm not allowed to stop outside the theatre. I've got into a lot of trouble recently for trying to do that. You can get out at Brammel Lane and it's just round the corner. You won't get lost.

[pause]

tone

[The recording is repeated.]

[pause]

Question 4   *Four*
In a hotel, the receptionist is giving a guest his bill. What is the problem?
A The man has made a mistake.
B It is someone else's bill.
C There is a mistake in the bill.

[pause]

tone

Receptionist: That's £125.97 altogether then, sir.
Guest: All right. Let me see. What's this? I'm sorry but, I made *one* phone call, not two. I've been charged for two calls. This is my bill, I suppose?
Receptionist: Why, yes, and the calls are automatically recorded by computer. I can't see how . . .
Guest: Oh, wait a minute. Yes, I did make a quick call to a friend last night. That would be it. Sorry.

[pause]

tone

[The recording is repeated.]

[pause]

Question 5   *Five*
You hear someone talking on a public phone. Who is he talking to?
A *a friend*
B *a repair man*
C *a taxi company*

[pause]

tone

Man: . . . look, you told me you'd pick me up in 10 to 15 minutes when I first rang but that was half an hour ago. I've been waiting outside this phone box all that time and it's freezing cold . . . What do you mean, it came and there was nobody here so it went away again? I've been here all the time, I haven't moved. Look, you're obviously unreliable, and I've got a plane to catch . . . No, no, I'll phone another firm.

[pause]

tone

[The recording is repeated.]

[pause]

Question 6   *Six*
In a museum café you overhear two people talking. What did the woman feel about the exhibition?
A *She was impressed.*
B *She was disappointed.*
C *She was bored.*

[pause]

tone

Female: . . . actually, it wasn't quite what I expected.
Man: Yes, I thought there'd be more variety.
Female: No, that's not what I meant. I didn't expect the colours to be so striking, it was so original.
Man: Yes, that's true – but the theme was so limited.
Female: I didn't mind. Where can I see more of his work?

[pause]

tone

[The recording is repeated.]

[pause]

Question 7   *Seven*
You hear a woman telephoning a furniture store. What does she want the store to do?
A *deliver her table on Tuesday*
B *leave the table at her neighbour's house*
C *confirm the delivery time*

[pause]

tone

Woman: Yes, good morning. I'm enquiring about the table I ordered a couple of weeks ago ... Mrs James, 58 West Street ... So when can you deliver it? ... Next Tuesday? OK ... No, hang on, that won't do ... Thursday? Should be OK. If I'm not here, my neighbour could let you in. Will it be morning or afternoon? ... Well, if you could let me know definitely ... Fine. Thank you ... Bye.

[pause]

tone

[The recording is repeated.]

[pause]

Question 8   *Eight*
You hear two people in a travel agent's arguing about a trip. What do they disagree about?
A whether to go or not
B how much it will cost
C when to go

[pause]

tone

Female: Look, I thought we'd agreed all this.
Male: Yes, but you heard what the assistant said – it can get unbearably hot there then.
Female: So what are you saying, you don't want to go? Look, I've already put my name down at work for those weeks and I don't want to have to change it.
Male: I'm just saying we shouldn't go *then*, that's all. It won't be any more expensive if we leave it until a bit later. Surely you could get them to put it back a bit ...

[pause]

tone

[The recording is repeated.]

[pause]

That is the end of Part One.

Now turn to Part Two.

PART 2   *You will hear part of a local radio programme, in which the presenters give the answers to a quiz. For questions 9 to 18, fill in the answers to the quiz.*

You now have forty-five seconds in which to look at Part Two.

[pause]

tone

Male:	. . . right, now it's time for the answers to last week's local history quiz. Carol, would you like to start?
Female:	OK, the first question was 'Who was Alexander Byfleet?' Did you know this one, Phil?
Male:	Well, I was sure he was an inventor. I didn't know we'd had any artists living here.
Female:	Well, that's what he was – painted some rather pretty pictures actually.
Male:	OK, next we asked you 'What used to be where the Buy Easy Supermarket is now?' There was some confusion over this one, wasn't there?
Female:	Mmm. Some people wrote the old police station and some said the old bus station, which is what it was. The old police station was further down the road.
Male:	The next question was 'Who was Jimmy Milburn, who lived here all his life?' This was a bit of a tricky one, wasn't it?
Female:	Yes, quite a few people fell into the trap and put 'professional footballer', but that was Johnny his brother.
Male:	In fact Jimmy was a golf champion – he won the national championships for five years running in the 1940s.
Female:	OK. Then we asked 'There was once a boot factory in the town. What is it now?' Not many people knew this one, did they?
Male:	No, including me! Well, apparently it was in Dean Road and when it closed it was used as a garage for a while before it became a furniture shop.
Female:	Which is what it currently is.
Male:	The next question was 'A hundred years ago, what was the town's main industry?' Well, the obvious answer was 'clothes-making' . . .
Female:	. . . yes, because of course that's what the town has a reputation for today. So it may come as a surprise to many of you that there was more engineering than anything else in those days . . .
Male:	. . . Uh huh.
Female:	We then asked 'What is the oldest building in the town?' A lot of you went for the Children's Hospital and, of course, the church. But, the church was completely rebuilt 150 years ago and the hospital is not quite as old as the Market Hall, which was built in 1672. Phil.
Male:	The next question was 'Anthony Diprose wrote a novel that was set in the town. What is that novel called?' Well, it wasn't a best seller so perhaps it's not so surprising that hardly anyone knew that the title of the book was 'Nothing Ever Changes'.
Female:	Then we asked 'What happened in Wood Lane in 1976 that was in all the national newspapers?' Well, plenty of people remembered there was a flood there in the mid-70s.
Male:	Yes, although as those of you who were actually living here in 1976 may recall, that was the year of our famous bank robbery . . .
Female:	The flood happened in '77 by the way.
Male:	The next question was 'Which public building was opened in 1985?' The new Town Hall was a popular answer and many of you put the Shopping Centre. Well, in fact they're both a bit older than that, believe it or not. It was the Leisure Centre that first came into use that year.
Female:	That surprised me. Anyway, finally, we asked 'What celebrates its hundredth anniversary this year?' The football club got a lot of votes here – it's been around longer than that! As many of you thought, it's our local newspaper, the Evening Post, which was first published 100 years ago.
Male:	OK, now for the winners.

[pause]

tone

Now you'll hear Part Two again.

[The recording is repeated.]

[pause]

That's the end of Part Two.

Now turn to Part Three.

PART 3   *You will hear five people talking on the radio about their jobs. For questions 19 to 23, choose from the list A to F how each got his or her job originally. Use the letters only once. There is one extra letter which you do not need to use.*

You now have thirty seconds in which to look at Part Three.

[pause]

tone

Speaker 1:   Well, I didn't really have the qualifications for the job, at least not on paper, but anyway, I got an interview, which was absolute hell, and afterwards I thought 'Well, it was worth a try', but I was sure I hadn't got it. Then, a couple of days later, they rang up and offered it to me. You know, it was only a few weeks later I found out that they'd intended to give it to someone else with the same surname, and I'd been second on the list. But I'm still there, so I suppose I'm OK.

[pause]

Speaker 2:   I've always loved selling and marketing and had several jobs doing that before this particular job. You know, it's strange how life is really because I very nearly didn't work here. Mr Kelly, he's the director, offered me the job at the interview, and I turned it down but he rang me again a few days later to see if I'd been having second thoughts. I had, I'm glad to say.

[pause]

Speaker 3:   My motorbike broke down. And I had to wait around while it was being repaired. Yeah, so I bought a local paper and went into a café and read it and happened to see the advert for the job. I thought, 'I'll have a go at that', and rang up. It was just down the road and they said, 'Come along right away'. I knew absolutely nothing about this line of work then, but they must have liked my face at the interview or something.

[pause]

Speaker 4:   Never be late for a job interview because you won't get the job! I ever so nearly was. Would you believe it? The train broke down on the way. There I was – stuck miles from where I was going. But actually we were in a station, and I realised I'd never make the interview and got off the train. Well, I got talking to someone outside and they offered me a lift and I arrived early for the interview, in the end.

[pause]

Speaker 5:   They rang up and offered me the job, and I was really thankful, because I'd been out of work for ages, and was beginning to think I'd never get anything. What I now know is that I was the only person who turned up for interview. Apparently a couple of other people were asked but never came. So I kind of got it because they had no choice, although they could have advertised it again, I suppose. Glad they didn't.

[pause]

tone

Now you'll hear Part Three again.

[The recording is repeated.]

[pause]

That's the end of Part Three.

Now turn to Part Four.

PART 4   *You will hear a young actress being interviewed on the radio. Answer questions 24 to 30, by writing T for True or F for False in the boxes provided.*

You now have thirty seconds in which to look at Part Four.

[pause]

tone

Interviewer: We have in the studio today, Beatrice Rand, a gifted young actress, well known to all of you for her starring role in *To Fly with the Wind* and whose next film is due out this summer.

Beatrice: Thank you.

Interviewer: I'd like to begin, if I may, by asking you about how it all started. Why an actress?

Beatrice: Oh, I've always wanted to be an actress. Or at least I've always wanted to perform. When I was very young, our neighbour used to play the piano all day every day. My parents hated it. They complained about it all the time. I couldn't understand why – I loved listening to him. It fascinated me. I wanted to be able to do it.

Interviewer: But you didn't start with music did you? In fact, wasn't your first love the circus?

Beatrice: Yes, my father made a circus area in our back garden with swings and ropes and things and I used to practise for hours. When I was seven I telephoned a circus school. They told me I had to wait until I was ten.

Interviewer: What did you do then?

Beatrice: For the time being I decided to be an actress. I was in all the school plays and I joined a local dramatic society – you know – only small things. I just wanted to perform. I used to imagine myself in front of huge audiences.

Interviewer: You had a very lively imagination when you were young.

Beatrice: Oh yes. I invented a completely imaginary life when I was about eight years old. And the most important part of my imaginary life was a friend called Elizabeth.

Interviewer: Do you think that was because you were lonely?

Beatrice: Not really. I had lots of school friends, but real friends can't be with you all the time. An imaginary friend can, and I could talk to Elizabeth whenever I wanted to. She was always there.

Interviewer: Did she encourage your desire to be an actress?

Beatrice:	Oh yes. She was always in the audience and she always told me when I'd done well and when I'd done badly.
Interviewer:	So by the time you left school you were already quite an experienced actress. In fact, at sixteen you were quite mature for your age.
Beatrice:	Yes, I suppose I was. I knew what I wanted to do when I was quite young and by the time I was sixteen I was well on the way to achieving it.
Interviewer:	Did you have any other interests when you were young?
Beatrice:	Well, I used to love reading. I read hundreds of books when I was young and I loved poetry. I knew a lot of poems by heart. I've always been very good at remembering words.
Interviewer:	And now that you're a successful actress, how do you feel about what you've achieved?
Beatrice:	I'm glad to be doing what I always wanted to do. But there are problems that I never thought about.
Interviewer:	Such as?
Beatrice:	Well, it's difficult to enjoy going to restaurants or discos and things like that. I wanted to improve my dancing. But going to dance classes wouldn't have been easy with everyone staring at you.
Interviewer:	And I believe your career is about to take another direction.

[pause]

tone

Now you'll hear Part Four again.

[The recording is repeated.]

[pause]

That's the end of Part Four.

There'll now be a pause of five minutes for you to copy your answers onto the separate answer sheet. I'll remind you when there is one minute left, so that you're sure to finish in time.

[pause]

You have one more minute left.

[pause]

That's the end of the test. Please stop now. Your supervisor will now collect all the question papers and answer sheets.
Goodbye.

Book 4 Test 3 Key

Paper 1 Reading (1 hour 15 minutes)

Part 1
1 E   2 H   3 G   4 C   5 D   6 A   7 B

Part 2
8 C   9 D   10 D   11 A   12 B   13 A   14 D   15 C

Part 3
16 G   17 E   18 B   19 F   20 A   21 C

Part 4
22 H   23 A   24 B   25 C   26 A   27 E   28 H   29 E
30/31 I/D (*in any order*)   32 G   33 F   34/35 A/F (*in any order*)

Paper 2 Writing (1 hour 30 minutes)

Task-specific mark schemes

Question 1
Content
Major points: State city to go to and when. Ask for a guide. Request information re being met at the airport and which hotel.
Minor points: Any requests for special arrangements. Any comment on spending allowance or meals.

Organisation and cohesion
Letter with appropriate opening and closing formulae. Clear organisation of points: statement of needs, questions and requests. Appropriate linking of ideas – not just lists.

Appropriacy of register and format
Letter format. Could range from neutral to formal, but must be consistent throughout.

Range
Language of requests and questions. Range of tenses: possibly future, present, conditionals. Vocabulary to do with travel and holidays. Some lifting of key words/phrases acceptable e.g. *special arrangements*.

Target reader
Would know what the writer specifically wants and have enough information to make the appropriate arrangements.

Question 2

Content
Give advice about how to learn the candidate's language. State main difficulties.
NB Also acceptable to expand on *one* main area of difficulty.

Range
Language for giving factual information, suggestions and advice. Probably present and future forms. Possibly conditionals and modals. Vocabulary to do with language learning.

Organisation and cohesion
Early reference to reason for writing. Clear organisation and linking of points. Suitable opening and closing formulae.

Appropriacy of register and format
Informal letter.

Target reader
Will have a clear idea as to how to start learning the language and what difficulties to expect.

Question 3

Content
Story which makes context of '*playing*' clear. What happened next, and with what result.

Range
Range of past tenses. Language of narration and description. Vocabulary appropriate to the context chosen.

Organisation and cohesion
Could be minimally paragraphed. Ideas linked and developed, leading from the given prompt to a specified outcome.

Appropriacy of register and format
Neutral or informal register possible, but must be consistent throughout.

Target reader
Would be able to follow the storyline.

Question 4

Content
Recommendations specific to a bookshop. Explanation as to why recommendations would prove popular with young people.

Range
Language of description and recommendation. Possibly present, future and conditionals. Vocabulary to do with shops and the likes or dislikes of young people.

Organisation and cohesion
Report should be clearly organised. Sub-headings an advantage. Report may possibly begin in letter format. Clearly stated recommendations.

Appropriacy of register and format
Register could range from neutral to formal, but must be consistent throughout.
Formal report layout not essential.

Target reader
Would have a clear idea of what the recommendations are and why they should
prove popular.

Question 5(a)

Content
State which book. Describe the scene. Explain why this scene is the one to film.

Range
Language of description, explanation and justification. Range of tenses.
Vocabulary relating to the specific scene chosen.

Organisation and cohesion
Logical linking between the description and the reasons for filming.

Appropriacy of register and format
Composition. Range of register appropriate, provided consistent.

Target reader
Would learn about the scene from the book in some detail and why it would be
good to film.

Question 5(b)

Content
State which book. Agree or disagree with the proposition, or discuss both sides
of the argument. Give reasons for the view. Explain this view with reference to
the book.

Range
Language of opinion, explanation, and justification. Range of tenses.
Vocabulary to do with books and language learning.

Organisation and cohesion
Clear development of viewpoint with appropriate linking of ideas.

Appropriacy of register and format
Composition. Range of register appropriate, provided consistent.

Target reader
Would know which book the writer had read and whether the reading of books
is seen as an aid to studying English.

Paper 3 Use of English (1 hour 15 minutes)

Part 1

1 B	2 A	3 A	4 B	5 A	6 B	7 C	8 D	9 C
10 A	11 C	12 D	13 D	14 B	15 A			

Part 2

16 it   **17** to   **18** they   **19** was   **20** a   **21** this/that   **22** have
23 for   **24** be   **25** than   **26** which/that   **27** as   **28** the
29 one   **30** had

Part 3

Award one mark for each correct section.
31 last time/occasion (when/that) (1) I saw (1)
32 is included (1) in (1)
33 taken the/his car (1) without asking (1)
34 had/'d better (1) get/have (1)
35 not like Sarah (1) to be (1)
36 want anyone/body else (1) to know (1)
37 was cancelled (1) owing to (1)
38 in case (1) the taxi is (1)
39 too fast/quickly (1) for them to (1)
40 gave me (1) (his/her) permission (1) OR gave (1) (his/her) permission for me (1)

Part 4

41 by   **42** of   **43** will   **44** ✓   **45** to   **46** the   **47** it
48 ✓   **49** ✓   **50** in   **51** ✓   **52** those   **53** quite
54 ✓   **55** other

Part 5

56 unemployment   **57** construction   **58** shortly
59 announcement(s)   **60** advertising   **61** qualified   **62** intention
63 recently   **64** enthusiastic   **65** wealthy

Paper 4   Listening (40 minutes approximately)

Part 1

1 C   **2** C   **3** A   **4** B   **5** A   **6** C   **7** C   **8** C

Part 2

9 camera equipment
10 up to 4/1–4/no more than 4/a max(imum) (of) 4/four
11 everyday objects *not* things like a bowl of fruit, etc.
12 (some)scenery/view(s) *not* view(s) from windows, etc.
13 comedy/amusing scenes (in home/at work)
14/15 (the/a)negative(s)/(a) (short) description (*in any order*)
16 Amateur Photography   **17** picture editor   **18** April (issue/magazine)

Part 3

19 B   **20** E   **21** A   **22** F   **23** C

Part 4

24 C   **25** N   **26** N   **27** B   **28** C   **29** C   **30** B

Transcript   *First Certificate Listening Test. Test Three.*
Hello. I'm going to give you the instructions for this test. I'll introduce each part of the test and give you time to look at the questions. At the start of each piece you'll hear this sound.

tone

You'll hear each piece twice.

Remember, while you're listening, write your answers on the question paper. You'll have time at the end of the test to copy your answers onto the separate answer sheet.

The tape will now be stopped. Please ask any questions now, because you must not speak during the test.

[pause]

PART 1   *Now open your question paper and look at Part One.*

[pause]

You will hear people talking in eight different situations. For questions 1 to 8, choose the best answer, A, B or C.

Question 1   *One*
Listen to this girl talking about a book she has just read. What does she think about the book?
A It is inaccurate.
B It is depressing.
C It is too long.

[pause]

tone

Woman: Hi, James. You can have your book back now. I finished it last night – finally. It took me ages to read. I liked the bits when he described his adventures in the mountains – they were really amazing. But I think he could have left out some of the descriptive passages. I'd have finished the book ages ago if he had.

[pause]

tone

[The recording is repeated.]

[pause]

Question 2   *Two*
You hear a woman talking to a man. What is she doing?

A *complaining about something*
B *suggesting something*
C *explaining something*

[pause]

Man:	Did you remember to bring the tennis balls?
Woman:	No, I didn't ...
Man:	What! I thought you said you'd bring some. How are we going to play without them?
Woman:	Well, the ones I had were very old and I know you'd only get cross if we played with them. So I phoned Janet. She's just bought some new tennis balls. She'll be along in a few minutes then we'll be able to play.

[pause]

tone

[The recording is repeated.]

[pause]

Question 3   *Three*
You overhear a woman talking about somewhere she visited on holiday.
What is she describing?
A *a palace*
B *an art gallery*
C *a department store*

[pause]

tone

Woman:	... oh yes, it was absolutely fascinating. They've got all these old family portraits on the walls and the rooms are full of beautiful furniture and, you know, exotic carpets and things. And there are vases and clocks and that sort of thing too ... Oh, and a marvellous collection of old toys on display in the royal nursery. I really liked that. You could just imagine the little princes and princesses playing with them. Then outside there was a ...

[pause]

tone

[The recording is repeated.]

[pause]

Question 4   *Four*
Listen to this couple talking about a parcel they have received. Why are they disappointed?
A *They ordered a different item.*
B *It is not suitable.*
C *It has been damaged.*

[pause]

tone

Woman:	Right, let's have a look. Oh no!
Man:	What's the matter? Faulty?
Woman:	This is no use.
Man:	Why?
Woman:	I *told* them over the phone what I needed it for and they said this one would do, but it obviously won't. Look!
Man:	Uhm. I see what you mean.

[pause]

tone

[The recording is repeated.]

[pause]

Question 5
Five
You hear a local shopkeeper talking about tourists. What is he complaining about?
A the way they treat local people
B the increasing numbers of them
C how little money they spend

[pause]

tone

Man: A few years ago there were hardly any, but now there are more and more every year. They've completely changed the place. I know the local economy couldn't do without them. And I don't mind them coming here, but the attitude of some of them gets on my nerves. They always argue about prices, they seem to think everything should be incredibly cheap. They get quite rude about it sometimes. They've no respect for us at all, some of them.

[pause]

tone

[The recording is repeated.]

[pause]

Question 6
Six
You switch on the radio and hear something being read. What is it?
A a weather forecast
B a news report
C a story

[pause]

tone

Man: . . . and with the wind roaring about his ears and the rain soaking his body, the weary traveller knocked on the door of the dark and unlit cottage. It was with a sinking heart that he waited. Then the door opened. A small elderly woman stood in front of him.

[pause]

tone

[The recording is repeated.]

[pause]

Question 7   *Seven*
You overhear two people talking as they leave their office. What is the
woman going to do this weekend?
A play tennis
B go to the beach
C work in the garden

[pause]

tone

Woman:	Bye, Mark! Have a nice weekend.
Man:	Thanks. Same to you. Doing anything exciting?
Woman:	No, not really. We were thinking of going down to the coast but I don't think Martin's going to be well enough, so he'll probably stay in and watch TV while I get on with planting the rose bushes I bought last weekend. How about you? Playing tennis again?

[pause]

tone

[The recording is repeated.]

[pause]

Question 8   *Eight*
You hear a man talking about his life. How does he feel?
A determined
B hopeful
C regretful

[pause]

tone

Male:	If I could, I would wish that I had a fairly decent job, payin' at least a hundred seventy five or two hundred dollars a week, a nice lady, somebody that would share my life with me, that I could talk to and be with, a place to stay, come home from work and watch TV – that's what I would wish for. Because you know when I was younger, I used to think that a lot of clothes and a lot of money was important. But now I realise that I ain't gonna live for ever so what good is a lot of money if I can't have happiness?

[pause]

tone

[The recording is repeated.]

[pause]

That is the end of Part One.
Now turn to Part Two.

PART 2   *You will hear a magazine editor talking on the radio about a competition. For questions 9 to 18, complete the notes.*

You now have thirty seconds in which to look at Part Two.

[pause]

tone

Announcer: And now it's time for our weekly magazine feature. I have with me Richard Stevens, editor of 'Amateur Photography'. Richard what's in this month's issue?

Richard: Thanks, Mary. Well, for all those listeners who are keen on taking photographs this may be the competition for you because you *could* win camera equipment to the value of £500 to take your next holiday shots with. Yes, that's first prize in our photography competition. So, here's what it's all about. We're asking anyone who's interested in taking part in this competition to send in up to four photographs. The photos must be five by eight inches – which is a bit larger than normal holiday snaps.

And it's not just any photograph that we're looking for. You must send photographs that fall into one of the following three categories. The first category is photographs of everyday objects – things like, an old chair, some brightly coloured cups and saucers or a bowl of fruit, for example. For the second category, you may choose to photograph some scenery, like the view from a window or a shot of the countryside or the sea. And lastly you could choose to send in a photograph for the comedy category – an amusing scene at work or in the home, for example. You can, of course, have people in these pictures but they won't be the main theme of the picture. So, those are the three types of photograph that you can send in and your entries can be in any of the three groups – there's no ruling about that. What we do insist on is that the pictures are taken by you and so we'll need the negative to prove that as well. And when you send in your entries, please also enclose a short description of the photos so that the judges can be sure of the subject matter and the category for each picture.

Now, you need to send the photographs to 'Amateur Photography' at 21, The Crescent, Ely. The telephone number is 243160 in case you need to ask for any extra information. When all the photographs have been received, they'll be judged during the first week of March by Miranda Smith, our picture editor. I'm afraid I can't give you any more information on that at the moment as we're still finalising details. So you've still got three weeks or so to take the pictures, or enlarge ones that you already have and send them in. The final date for entries is the last day of February and the winners will be announced in our April issue.

Announcer: So what else have you got this month, Richard?

Richard: Well, we've got a special feature . . .

[pause]

tone

Now you'll hear Part Two again.

[The recording is repeated.]

[pause]

That's the end of Part Two.
Now turn to Part Three.

PART 3   *You will hear five different women talking about the activities they enjoy.*
          For questions 19 to 23, choose from the list A to F what each speaker says
          about her activity. Use the letters only once. There is one extra letter which
          you do not need to use.

          You now have thirty seconds in which to look at Part Three.

          [pause]

          tone

Speaker 1:   Well, I suppose I really took up yoga when I left school because there – at school, I
              mean – they made us take part in all these team games and well, you know it was all
              about who won and who was best. That's not really me. I was looking for something
              more . . . um . . . well, more individual really, where I could work within my own limits
              and not be obliged to compete all the time. So, I can just shut myself away in my
              room and get on with it.

Speaker 2:   Yes, what I really like about cycling is getting out into the countryside at the
              weekends and just riding along in the fresh air. I sometimes go for miles, not really
              thinking about anything. I find it quite restful in a way, you know, just getting away
              from the stress of living and working in a big city. We often go as a family – me, my
              husband and the three children – I think it's a good family activity. And then, well, by
              Monday morning I'm all refreshed and ready for work again.

Speaker 3:   Well, I usually go swimming two or three evenings a week, you know, after work,
              sometimes I go with colleagues and sometimes on my own. It keeps me fit, you
              know, and reasonably slim. I learnt when I was about five and I loved it, and I've
              always kept it up. I think it's something that everybody should learn, whether you
              want to win races or just get a bit of exercise.

Speaker 4:   Mountaineering always attracted me, even as a child, maybe because where we lived
              was really flat. I've always dreamed of climbing Mount Everest one day – I suppose
              all climbers see that as the ultimate challenge. The highest I've been so far since I
              started climbing at the university was last year when I went to South America. It was
              fantastic. The great thing is everyone has a part to play. Everyone has to rely on
              everyone else and you all work together to get to the top.

Speaker 5:   I only started skiing about three years ago, so I'm not very good yet. I love getting up
              into the mountains, especially early in the morning before there are too many people
              about and the snow's still fresh. Later in the day's fun too but in a different way, but
              that first ski of the day is always special. Of course, one of the great things about
              skiing is there's always plenty to do in the evenings and it's very easy to make
              friends. I enjoy the company. I just wish I could afford to go more often!

          [pause]

          tone

          Now you'll hear Part Three again.

[The recording is repeated.]

[pause]

That's the end of Part Three.
Now turn to Part Four.

PART 4   *You'll hear a conversation in which Alan asks his friends Bob and Carol about a sports club. Answer questions 24 to 30 by writing B for Bob, C for Carol, or N for Neither in the boxes provided.*

You now have thirty seconds in which to look at Part Four.

[pause]

tone

Alan: That sports club you both belong to, what's it like Bob?

Bob: Not bad actually.

Alan: What can you do there?

Bob: Oh, the usual things, squash, tennis, swimming pool, fitness classes, all that.

Carol: But then there are the things you don't find everywhere, like indoor golf and yoga . . .

Bob: Yeah, but Carol you don't . . .

Carol: Yeah, there's not a lot of variety in what I do. I mean, I keep meaning to take up some of the other things, but basically I just use the swimming pool.

Alan: Doesn't sound bad from what you're saying.

Bob: Yeah, but I must say some of the equipment has seen better days. I was in the gym the other day using the weights and . . . well . . . a fair amount of the stuff in there isn't exactly the most up to date.

Carol: I wouldn't know about that . . . I never use it. But you can't really expect perfection for what we pay.

Alan: I meant to ask you about that, because I'm thinking of joining.

Bob: Well, they've just put the membership fees up. I don't mind paying a bit more, though . . . it's still quite reasonable, considering what you get.

Carol: Yeah, these places can be quite expensive from what I've seen advertised. This has gone up a bit . . . it could be a lot worse, though. I could find out for you how much it is for new members now.

Alan: What kind of people go there?

Bob: All sorts. I've met all kinds of people I wouldn't normally run into. There are people of all ages and incomes but everyone gets on well. It doesn't really matter how well off you are when you're running round a tennis court, does it? It can be rather competitive but we also have a laugh a lot of the time.

Carol: I'm sure I could make friends if I put a bit more effort in. But there isn't a lot of talking in the swimming pool – most people stay on their own or with their own friends. There isn't a lot of mixing in my experience.

Alan: Actually, I was thinking of taking up some serious fitness training – what are the instructors like?

Bob: I did a bit of that but I gave it up. It was too much like hard work. The instructors never lost patience with me. Though to be honest I wouldn't blame them if they had. You're supposed to be keen if you take those classes and I was a bit lazy.

Carol: I did some aqua classes once – that's various kinds of exercises in the water – but I gave it up. They weren't bad, but I got the feeling that the instructors were just there for the money. They didn't take much interest in us. You didn't get any individual attention, which is what I wanted.

Alan: Well, how about the changing rooms and things like that?

Bob: I've never found the changing rooms I use anything other than spotless, I must say. And the showers, well, I've seen better. But they'll do.

Carol: The changing room I use – the one for the swimming pool – can be pretty mucky. People mention it and they do something about it for a while. But it doesn't last. As for the showers, well, all I'll say is I get in and out as fast as I can.

Alan: Well, maybe I'll join – I probably wouldn't use the pool much anyway.

Bob: We could take you as a guest – guests are free for up to three visits.

Alan: Oh.

Carol: Yeah, why don't you come on Tuesday and see for yourself? We could go for a drink in the Sports Bar Café afterwards.

Alan: Thanks.

Bob: Yeah, that's just opened. It's really convenient to be able to go and have something to eat and drink when you've finished. I thought they were building a bigger place, though. It gets pretty crowded and it can take ages to get served.

Carol: Yeah, but come on! Before that there wasn't anything except a couple of drinks machines. It was really awful. The place really needed something like the new café.

Alan: OK, I'll come on Tuesday.

[pause]

tone

Now you'll hear Part Four again.

[The recording is repeated.]

[pause]

That's the end of Part Four.
There'll now be a pause of five minutes for you to copy your answers onto the separate answer sheet. I'll remind you when there is one minute left, so that you're sure to finish in time.

[pause]

You have one more minute left.

[pause]

That's the end of the test. Please stop now. Your supervisor will now collect all the question papers and answer sheets.
Goodbye.

Book 4 Test 4 Key

Paper 1 Reading (1 hour 15 minutes)

Part 1
1 F   2 A   3 E   4 G   5 H   6 C   7 B

Part 2
8 B   9 A   10 D   11 A   12 C   13 B   14 A   15 D

Part 3
16 C   17 A   18 F   19 D   20 B   21 E

Part 4
22 B   23 C   24 A   25 B   26 C   27 D   28 C   29 D
30 C   31 A   32 B   33 C   34 D   35 D

Paper 2 Writing (1 hour 30 minutes)

Task-specific mark schemes

Question 1
Content
Major points: All 6 points to be covered. Give brief details of requirements:
room for 30 people, date, time. Ask about: meal, drinks and disco.
Minor points: Possible request for vegetarian meal. Any additional information.

Organisation and cohesion
Early reference to why the person is writing. Grouping of ideas into sections
giving information and requesting information. Suitable opening and closing
formulae.
Not just a list of questions, *unless* the list is introduced appropriately.

Appropriacy of register and format
Letter format. Consistently neutral or formal.

Range
Language appropriate for giving and seeking factual information, and making
requests. Present and future forms. Vocabulary to do with arranging a party.
Lifting of key words permissible e.g. *disco, meal.*

Target reader
Would be aware of the writer's requirements and be able to respond to
questions.

Question 2

Content

Description of *one* special day of a holiday abroad, and an explanation of why it was so exciting (special).

Range

Descriptive and narrative language. Language of explanation. Past tenses.

Organisation and cohesion

Though an article, as a piece of narrative writing it could be minimally paragraphed. There should be a clear link between narration, description and explanation.

Appropriacy of register and format

Range of register is allowable, provided consistent.

Target reader

Would understand why the day was exciting (special).

Question 3

Content

Composition could agree or disagree with the proposition, or discuss both sides of the argument. Should give *some* examples from present and/or past to back up opinion.

Range

Language of comparison and description, opinion and justification. Probably past and present tenses.

Organisation and cohesion

Clear presentation and development of ideas, stating writer's point of view. Appropriate linking of ideas.

Appropriacy of register and format

Neutral composition format.

Target reader

Would be able to understand the writer's viewpoint.

Question 4

Content

State benefits to writer's town – at least *one* each for both park and museum. Statement of preference: clear choice. Reason for preference.

Range

Language of description, comparison, preference, opinion and justification. Present and future tenses (perhaps conditionals and modals).

Organisation and cohesion

Report should be clearly organised. Sub-headings an advantage.

Appropriacy of register and format

Neutral or formal, but must be consistent. Formal report layout not essential.

Target reader
Would understand the choice the writer would make and the writer's reasons for it.

Question 5(a)

Content
Composition could agree or disagree with the proposition, or discuss both sides of the argument. Must refer to the ending in the chosen book.

Range
Language of description, opinion and justification. Range of tenses.

Organisation and cohesion
Clear presentation and development of ideas, including a statement of the writer's point of view. Appropriate linking of description and comment.

Appropriacy of register and format
Neutral composition.

Target reader
Would understand the writer's view of the ending.

Question 5(b)

Content
Make recommendation to read the named book, and give more than one reason for this recommendation. Must *clearly* relate to the book chosen.

Range
Language of description, encouragement, persuasion and justification. Range of tenses.

Organisation and cohesion
Informal letter, with suitable opening and closing formulae, and early reference to reason for writing. Clear presentation and development of ideas. Appropriate linking of recommendation and reasons.

Appropriacy of register and format
Informal letter.

Target reader
Would learn something about the book and why the writer is recommending it. Would want to read the book.

Paper 3   Use of English (1 hour 15 minutes)

Part 1

1 B	2 C	3 A	4 D	5 C	6 B	7 D	8 D	9 A
10 C	11 B	12 D	13 A	14 B	15 C			

Part 2

16 that/which   **17** be   **18** the   **19** part/role   **20** without
21 of   **22** all   **23** sure/certain   **24** run/sell   **25** so
26 are/get   **27** lot   **28** with   **29** aside/away   **30** not/never

Part 3

Award one mark for each correct section.
31 would/'d/should (1) 've/have sent (1)
32 too tired (1) to eat (1)
33 to put (1) up with (1)
34 you mind (1) lending me (1)
35 was not/wasn't allowed (1) to stay (1)
36 did it take (1) (you) to (1)
37 haven't/have not (1) been skiing for (1) OR haven't/have not (1) skied for (1)
38 although (s)he (1) isn't/is not able/is unable (1)
39 are (being) bought (1) by teenagers (1)
40 wish I hadn't/had not (1) invited (1)

Part 4

41 it   **42** being   **43** for   **44** ✓   **45** her   **46** at   **47** to
48 ourselves   **49** ✓   **50** that   **51** ✓   **52** of   **53** ✓
54 our   **55** the

Part 5

56 competition   **57** performance   **58** nervous   **59** successful
60 thoroughly   **61** activity   **62** carefully   **63** imprisoned
64 political   **65** explanation

Paper 4   Listening (40 minutes approximately)

Part 1

1 A   **2** B   **3** A   **4** B   **5** A   **6** B   **7** C   **8** C

Part 2

 9 five/5 (years old)
10 Winter Olympics/Winter Olympic Games
11 North America/Canada (in particular)
12 this season/this year/recently   **13** $3\frac{1}{2}$/three and a half months
14 stay (here/there/in Canada)   **15** most important match/game
16 (the) champion(s)
17 (first team) place/place (in the first team) *not* first place
18 (a) holiday (in Finland)

Part 3

19 F   **20** D   **21** C   **22** E   **23** A

Part 4
24 B   25 A   26 C   27 A   28 B   29 A   30 A

Transcript   *First Certificate Listening Test. Test Four.*

Hello. I'm going to give you the instructions for this test. I'll introduce each part of the test and give you time to look at the questions. At the start of each piece you'll hear this sound.

tone

You'll hear each piece twice.

Remember, while you're listening, write your answers on the question paper. You'll have time at the end of the test to copy your answers onto the separate answer sheet.

The tape will now be stopped. Please ask any questions now, because you must not speak during the test.

[pause]

PART 1   *Now open your question paper and look at Part One.*

[pause]

You will hear people talking in eight different situations. For questions 1 to 8, choose the best answer, A, B or C.

Question 1   One
Listen to these people talking about an event. What event are they talking about?
A a concert
B a play
C a film

[pause]

tone

Man:	Great, wasn't it!
Woman:	Well, it was OK. I thought the sound could have been a lot better.
Man:	Yeah – but it was just great being there – the atmosphere was incredible.
Woman:	Well, I thought it was too crowded and the guy next to me kept waving his arms about. He really got on my nerves.
Man:	Well, I thought it was brilliant. If they're playing again next month, I'll definitely go again.

[pause]

tone

[The recording is repeated.]

[pause]

Question 2   Two
You hear someone talking about a party he has been invited to. How does he
feel about the party?
A He is nervous about it.
B He thinks it will be boring.
C He is unsure what to expect.

[pause]

tone

Male:	I must admit that I'm not really looking forward to it . . .
Female:	No?
Male:	Well, I've been to their parties before and I don't suppose this one'll be any better . . . all the same people going on and on about their jobs.
Female:	Uh huh
Male:	– they all think they're so important . . . honestly, I just can't face them, I never know what to say! Still I've been invited so I suppose I'd better go.
Female:	Mmm

[pause]

tone

[The recording is repeated.]

[pause]

Question 3   Three
You hear this radio announcement about driving conditions. What is the
main danger tonight?
A ice
B snow
C floods

[pause]

tone

Announcer:	With the bad weather continuing, problems are also continuing on the roads. Although river levels have started to fall and further flooding is now unlikely, we are faced tonight with falling temperatures which, combined with wet roads from the earlier flooding, will lead to ice on the roads. The colder weather does mean, however, that there will be little in the way of rain or snow tonight, apart from the odd shower here and there.

[pause]

tone

[The recording is repeated.]

[pause]

Question 4   *Four*
You hear part of a radio play. Where is the scene taking place?
A on a beach
B in a hotel
C in a restaurant

[pause]

tone

Man:	I don't feel too good. I think I might have overdone the sunbathing today.
Woman:	I did warn you – you're not used to all this heat. So, what about dinner?
Man:	I couldn't face anything just now. I think I'll stay in and lie down for a while.
Woman:	You'll probably feel better in a bit. Shall I meet you down here, by the lift, later on then? Maybe we could go to that little place just down the street.
Man:	OK, if I'm feeling better.

[pause]

tone

[The recording is repeated.]

[pause]

Question 5   *Five*
Listen to this woman telling a friend about a television series. What is her opinion of it?
A It is highly original.
B It is very well acted.
C It is the best series on TV.

[pause]

tone

Woman:	I didn't know what to make of it at first but I really like it now. To be honest some of the acting is a bit, well, unconvincing ... but that's not the point. The stories are so clever ... completely unlike any of that usual detective stuff. You know, in other series the detective always solves the crime. But in this one ... sometimes that doesn't happen. It's one of the programmes I try not to miss.

[pause]

tone

[The recording is repeated.]

[pause]

Question 6   *Six*
You hear someone talking about a hotel. Who is the speaker?
A a hotel receptionist
B a hotel manager
C a hotel chef

[pause]

tone

Man: When I started there, well ... it had been run really badly. The kitchens ... oh dear ... shocking, the waiters and waitresses they were so awful to guests ... constant complaints about the food. The administration ... it was terrible – when guests came to reception they were lucky if anyone could be bothered to deal with them at all. Well, it's all different now – I got rid of a few people ... organised staff training ... anyone can see the whole place is much more efficient now.

[pause]

tone

[The recording is repeated.]

[pause]

Question 7   *Seven*
You hear a British actress, Melina Morton, talking on the radio. Why does Melina live in the USA?
A Her friends are there.
B It's good for her job.
C To be with her husband.

[pause]

tone

Actress: I spend most of my time in the USA these days, we have a house in Connecticut. But, I do get homesick, I love to come home and, luckily, in my job, I seem to be able to once or twice a year because I miss my friends, you know, I miss walking around London and it's ... well, you know if you're born in a place, you always want to come back, at least I know I do. But, since my husband, Mike, has a theatre school, he's a drama and singing coach, and, of course, it was much easier for me to get on a plane and go somewhere to work, than to ask Mike to, you know, suddenly close down the thriving school and try to open one here, you know, it was just not on to do that.

[pause]

tone

[The recording is repeated.]

[pause]

Question 8   *Eight*
You hear someone talking in a tourist information centre. What is the situation?
A She has just arrived in the town.
B She can't find her hotel.
C She has no place to stay.

[pause]

tone

Woman: . . . so I told them that I wanted the room for another few days but it wasn't possible. I should have told them before, I left it until too late. Anyway, I packed my things and today I've been all over the place, up and down the streets for hours and hours, asking everywhere but I haven't had any success. There aren't any others in my guidebook. So is there anywhere else I can try? I've really enjoyed my time here so far, and I don't want to leave if I can avoid it. Can you help me?

[pause]

tone

[The recording is repeated.]

[pause]

That is the end of Part One.
Now turn to Part Two.

PART 2 *You will hear part of a radio interview with Mikko Korhonen, a Finnish ice hockey star. For questions 9 to 18, complete the sentences which summarise what the ice hockey star says.*

You now have forty-five seconds in which to look at Part Two.

[pause]

tone

Interviewer: Mikko Korhonen is the latest European ice hockey star to cross the Atlantic and join a major team in North America. He left his native Finland to live here in Quebec, in Canada, where he now plays in the National Hockey League. So, Mikko, why did you come all the way to Canada?

Mikko: Well, playing in the National League – the NHL – was a dream I'd had since I was . . . I don't know . . . since I saw my first game . . . I must've been, what, five, I suppose. The only thing that came close to being able to play in the National League was getting the bronze medal for Finland in the Winter Olympics.

The sport in Europe is getting better – the facilities in some places are excellent now and more people are taking an interest – but North America, and Canada in particular, is where it's happening. That's why so many Scandinavians and Russians come here to play. Mind you it took me ages to break into the first team – I didn't manage it until this season. The first game for my Quebec team was incredible. I've been here for four years and I'd given myself until this season to get a first team place. If I hadn't, I'd have given up and gone back to Finland.

Interviewer: But it nearly didn't happen?

Mikko: No, no, that's right. The NHL got involved in an argument with the players and the television companies over money and the team manager stopped all games at national level for three and a half months. You can imagine how I felt! I'd finally been offered the chance to play in a big team and then, just at the start of the season, everything stopped. They were the most depressing months of my life. A lot of players went over to Europe to play, but I thought it would be better for me to stay here.

Interviewer: And now, finally, your dream's come true.

148

Mikko:	Yeah. For the last four weeks I've been playing here in Quebec and we've hardly lost a game. We've got our most important match early in April. The other team have always been stronger in the past, but this year things are different. We could actually be the champions for the first time in ten years. I can't wait – it'll be a great game! Imagine being in a cup-winning side in my first real season!
	Everybody seems to be scoring at the moment and my main worry now is keeping my first team place. I haven't got long to prove my worth. My contract's only for one year to begin with, so I'll have to work pretty hard. How I do now will decide my whole future. If everything goes OK, well, I've got a girlfriend here, so I guess if it all works out, I'd like to make my home here permanently. Who knows? – maybe one day my children will play for Canada in the Olympics! Mind you, whatever happens this season, I'm planning a holiday in Finland at the end of it.
Interviewer:	Well, thank you, Mikko, and best of luck for the rest of the season!
Mikko:	Thank you.
Interviewer:	And now we move on to rugby . . .

[pause]

tone

Now you'll hear Part Two again.

[The recording is repeated.]

[pause]

That's the end of Part Two.
Now turn to Part Three.

PART 3   *You will hear five people talking about their jobs. For questions 19 to 23, choose which of the opinions A to F each speaker expresses. Use the letters only once. There is one extra letter which you do not need to use.*

You now have thirty seconds in which to look at Part Three.

[pause]

tone

Speaker 1:	Well, being a hotel receptionist suits me down to the ground . . . I mean, I never dreamt I'd end up doing so little but getting a decent salary! I thought when I started that it was going to be a struggle to keep up with everything but it's turned out to be absolutely ideal. There's nothing I can't deal with and some days I'm even looking for things to do! I'm not sure if it's always going to be like that but right now I just can't believe my luck!
Speaker 2:	I might not be making much at the moment but I reckon I will be before too long. You know, the other day, the boss came up to me and said, 'Carry on like this and you'll really go places here. You've got a real gift for selling on the phone.' Well, I was pretty busy at the time and I didn't take it in till I got home and then I thought, 'Nobody in that place has ever said anything like that to me before. I could be on my way up!'
Speaker 3:	What's really different about *this* computing job for me is that, for once, I don't have anyone breathing down my neck all the time. I just get on with my own thing in my own room without anyone bothering me. I've got a lot of responsibility actually, and I

149

have to watch what decisions I make, but at least I don't have people criticising me all day. Of course, I don't get involved in the office gossip, but well, I don't really miss all that.

Speaker 4: I know this might sound daft, because the job itself is actually rather dull, but I can't wait to go in there in the morning. It doesn't take me long to get there and the journey back's just as quick, but what I really like is how much fun the others are. I know it's not what I'd planned to do, working in a fast food restaurant, and I might not end up doing it for long, but we have such a laugh that it makes up for how boring the work is.

Speaker 5: What appeals to me is that I never know what's going to come up from one day to the next. Sometimes there's not that much on and I can get away early, and other times it's frantic and I have to stay on late. It's certainly good experience if I want to go to a bigger travel agency one day, but I've no plans to at the moment. I mean, there's always something new to learn, something unexpected to deal with.

[pause]

tone

Now you'll hear Part Three again.

[The recording is repeated.]

[pause]

That's the end of Part Three.
Now turn to Part Four.

PART 4 *You will hear an interview about adventure sports. For questions 24 to 30, choose the best answer, A, B or C.*

You now have one minute in which to look at Part Four.

[pause]

tone

Interviewer: ... Welcome back to the programme. Well, statistics show that the fastest growing sports in Britain are adventure sports and I have with me Stan Leach, an official at the Sports Council, who's going to tell us a bit about some of them. Stan, where shall we start?

Stan: Well, most people start with walking, I think – although of course strictly speaking it's not necessarily an adventure sport, but it's what gets most people outdoors. Indeed, the great thing about walking in Britain is the endless variety, from an easy stroll to a country pub to an energetic walk up a high peak. If you want to take up walking, you can start with a few short circular walks and then pick something longer and more demanding.

Interviewer: What's this thing called scrambling I've been hearing about?

Stan: Yeah, scrambling is sort of in the grey area between walking and climbing. Scrambles are graded according to difficulty, and on the harder ones, which are quite close to rock climbing, it's best to go with an expert.

Interviewer: Well, that brings us nicely on to climbing – that's really caught on here lately, hasn't it?

Stan: Yes, and of course you know it doesn't have to mean going up the really big ones like Everest. Climbing might seem rather terrifying to begin with, but it's great fun and really keeps you fit. You start by climbing small crags before moving on to a rock face. I went for a day's lesson with mountaineer Alan Kimber in Scotland and it was really scary but really exciting.

Interviewer: Right, well, what's next?

Stan: Mountain biking. If you can get used to the saddle, you can cycle across Britain, but unlike in the USA, where there are special cycling paths, in Britain most of the paths are the same as for walkers, which can cause a bit of trouble. After the initial investment – there's one bike that costs £4,000 but you can get a very good one for £200 – it's a cost efficient sport. And there are relatively easy trips such as the Pyrenees Traverse which has 70% downhill slopes with no major climbs.

Interviewer: Scuba diving's my personal favourite – any advice on that?

Stan: Yes, swimming underwater opens up a whole new world. Actually, for most people, the idea of being underwater, unable to breathe normally, is a frightening one, but with good tuition you can pick it up in no time at all. Once you get the qualification you need to be considered a competent diver, you can do it anywhere.

Interviewer: I see you've got skydiving on your list. Surely that's only for people who are very brave or mad?

Stan: Well, it is the sort of thing you'd expect to only see in the movies but you'd be amazed how many people go in for it these days. Six hours of training will give you enough background to make the first jump. People who really take to it often join display teams, so if you take it up you might find yourself taking part in special events.

Interviewer: OK, and finally canoeing. That always looks a bit dangerous to me – in that tiny boat with water rushing everywhere.

Stan: Well, there are some terrible bits of water where the real canoeing experts go but beginners can start in gentler waters and build up. There's one stretch in Wales that was designed for the world championships that has a dam release, so that at pre-set times the water runs through. You can phone up and they'll say it's a full release tomorrow or a quarter release, so you can choose your times according to difficulty.

Interviewer: OK, Stan, thanks a lot. After the break, we'll be going to Canada to look at . . .

[pause]

tone

Now you'll hear Part Four again.

[The recording is repeated.]

[pause]

That's the end of Part Four.
There'll now be a pause of five minutes for you to copy your answers onto the separate answer sheet. I'll remind you when there is one minute left, so that you're sure to finish in time.

[pause]

You have one more minute left.

[pause]

That's the end of the test. Please stop now. Your supervisor will now collect all the question papers and answer sheets.
Goodbye.